ALSO BY MICHAEL TOUGIAS

Overboard!:
A True Blue-water Odyssey of Disaster and Survival

Fatal Forecast:
An Incredible True Tale of Disaster and Survival at Sea

Ten Hours Until Dawn:
The True Story of Heroism and Tragedy Aboard the Can Do

The Finest Hours:
The True Story of the U.S. Coast Guard's Most Daring Sea Rescue
(coauthor Casey Sherman)

Until I Have No Country:
A Novel of King Philip's War

River Days:
Exploring the Connecticut River from Source to Sea

King Philip's War:
The History and Legacy of America's Forgotten Conflict
(coauthor Eric Schultz)

Quabbin:
A History and Explorers Guide

The Blizzard of '78

There's a Porcupine in My Outhouse:
Misadventures of a Mountain Man Wannabe

AMC's Best Day Hikes Near Boston
(coauthor John Burke)

A STORM TOO SOON

A TRUE STORY OF DISASTER, SURVIVAL, AND AN INCREDIBLE RESCUE

MICHAEL J. TOUGIAS

SCRIBNER

New York   London   Toronto   Sydney   New Delhi

SCRIBNER
A Division of Simon & Schuster, Inc.
1230 Avenue of the Americas
New York, NY 10020

First Scribner hardcover edition January 2013

SCRIBNER and design are registered trademarks of The Gale Group, Inc.,
used under license by Simon & Schuster, Inc., the publisher of this work.

For information about special discounts for bulk purchases,
please contact Simon & Schuster Special Sales at 1-866-506-1949
or business@simonandschuster.com.

The Simon & Schuster Speakers Bureau can bring authors to your live event.
For more information or to book an event contact the Simon & Schuster Speakers Bureau
at 1-866-248-3049 or visit our website at www.simonspeakers.com.

Manufactured in the United States of America

1   3   5   7   9   10   8   6   4   2

Library of Congress Control Number: 2012038583

ISBN 978-1-4516-8333-2
ISBN 978-1-4516-8335-6 (ebook)

To Paul and Jane Lorraine, and Alison O'Leary

CONTENTS

PART I

PART II

2792

CONTENTS

PART III

PART I

CHAPTER ONE

FLORIDA – COUNTDOWN TO THE CROSSING

The flight from Ottawa to Florida is a long one, but Rudy Snel doesn't mind as he gazes out the aircraft window at the clouds below. He's thinking about the next leg of his trip: a voyage on the *Sean Seamour II*—a forty-four-foot sailboat—that will carry him and two others from Florida to the Azores, then on to Gibraltar and Saint-Tropez. Sailing across the Atlantic has been a dream of Rudy's since he was nine years old when his family emigrated from Holland to Canada crossing the Atlantic on a passenger ship. In the course of the voyage they encountered a storm that caused the ocean liner to pitch and roll, making just about everyone on board seasick. But not Rudy. He was out on the top deck in the pelting rain having the time of his life, awed by the raging sea around him.

Rudy is now sixty-two years old and recently retired from a teaching career in the public schools. He finally has the time to live out his dream of returning to the sea. A five-foot-nine-inch Canadian with gray hair and a neatly trimmed beard, he is an adventurous soul; the hardships expected on a transatlantic crossing don't bother him in the least. He owns his own sailboat and often sails the Ottawa River, but he has also mastered piloting small aircraft and parachuting. He has made more than six hundred parachute jumps. On one of those jumps, his parachute did not deploy properly, and when he looked up at the tangled mess during his free fall, his reaction wasn't one of alarm, but of annoyance. He would have to pull his reserve parachute, and was already thinking ahead to the considerable effort it would take to repack it. He landed safely.

When he saw a notice on a website announcing that a crew was needed for a transatlantic crossing, he was able to tell the captain that while his sailing experience was limited to inland waterways, he wasn't prone to panic when the unexpected happened. He was capable of standing watch and had never been motion-sick in his life. He explained that he wanted to go on the voyage to learn about blue-water sailing and because it would be an entirely new experience. He didn't retire from his job just to sit around and grow soft.

When the plane touches down in Jacksonville, Florida, Rudy disembarks and follows the crowd down to baggage claim. He is met by the captain, fifty-seven-year-old Jean Pierre de Lutz, who goes by the nickname JP. The two men shake hands and then head outside. The warm, humid air embraces Rudy, a welcome change from the cold of Ottawa. It is late April, the temperature is in the mid-eighties, and the brilliant sunshine causes Rudy to squint.

They drive directly to the *Sean Seamour II,* which is moored at Green Cove Springs on the St. Johns River. Rudy likes what he sees. The Beneteau sailboat has a center cockpit protected by a hard dodger (rigid windshield), a single mast directly in front of the cockpit, with twin guardrails surrounding the white vessel. During inclement weather, the cockpit can be completely enclosed with canvas curtains and windows. It's a sleek-looking boat—Rudy thinks it's beautiful.

The third crew member, Ben Tye, emerges from the boat's cabin. Jean Pierre introduces the thirty-one-year-old sailor to Rudy. Ben is British, with a short, stocky build and a shaved head. He began his career in the tourism industry, but he soon turned his interest to the sea, first teaching inshore sailing on small vessels, and then progressing to yacht deliveries. Now working toward his yachtmaster captain's license, he is focused on gaining more miles at sea. He has sailed from Europe to the United States, and on this trip he will reverse course. Reserved by nature, Ben tends to take time before opening up, but that night at dinner, he already feels comfortable and is more than satisfied that the threesome will make a good crew. He is impressed that JP has spared no expense in equipping the boat and is taking his time readying it for the crossing. In his quiet manner, JP patiently explains the intricacies of his vessel, and Ben senses that this is a man who never gets rattled.

Ben and Rudy don't know it, but JP had more than a dozen candidates answer his request for a crew. He interviewed each applicant, narrowing them down to two crew members, relying on his instincts to determine who would be the best fit. He was more than sure that Rudy and Ben were the right men for the job. JP selected May as the optimal time of year for an eastbound crossing of the Atlantic, primarily because it would put them ahead of hurricane season. He'd had a brush with a hurricane in a prior crossing and wanted no part of another.

The voyage is not scheduled for another few days because the *Sean Seamour II* was in storage for two and a half years, and needs a complete overhaul, cleaning, and provisioning. Some of the equipment was removed and stored in an air-conditioned warehouse. Now that equipment needs to be inspected, replaced if necessary, and secured in its proper position aboard the boat. Rudy and Ben will work under JP's supervision. Each man will have a private berth; Ben's will be the forward cabin, Rudy's the stern, and JP's the port side, closest to the chart table and the companionway leading up to the cockpit. As they start taking apart the inside of the boat and checking equipment, JP realizes that time and climate have done their share of damage. They order a new wind sensor, cable replacements for the mast, autopilot hydraulic pump, new fuel filters, and a new battery bank. The fuel tank is cleaned and a custom-made auxiliary tiller packed in case of emergency. New life jackets and flares are stowed. JP replaces the navigation and electronics by installing the latest MaxSea weather routing software, which will enable him to receive detailed wind data several days in advance, allowing him to adjust course accordingly. A backup computer with navigation and satellite telephone software is also on board and in working order.

The preparation introduces Ben and Rudy to the inner workings of the boat as they replace lines, clean equipment, and practice using the pumps. As the two men lay out the drogues and their lines on the dock, Ben says, "I hope we won't need them." Rudy counters, "Well, I'd like to see a bit of heavy weather, just for the experience."

The life raft and GPIRB (global position indicating radio beacon, which can send a signal to the Coast Guard, pinpointing the location of an emergency) went out for recertification, and the entire crew reviews their operation before securing the two pieces of safety equipment. The GPIRB is one step advanced from the traditional EPIRB (emergency position indicating radio beacon) because it has an integrated GPS that gives the receiver, the Coast Guard, a faster location fix and does not require the receiver to perform any complex calculations. The GPIRB on the *Sean Seamour II* is mounted in its cradle inside the cabin for ready access.

Also on board is an older EPIRB from an earlier boat of JP's. Although it is a somewhat redundant piece of equipment, JP has tested its eleven-year-old batteries and the unit works, so he decides to keep it on board. He installs the EPIRB in its cradle on the inside of the cockpit's hard dodger, where it is safe from sea spray and wash-downs. The EPIRB does not have a hydrostatic release, but its signal is water-activated, and the captain doesn't want any false alarms.

JP reviews the heavy-weather contingencies with the crew, making sure they understand exactly what needs to be dogged down in a storm. They examine the location and operation of all safety equipment. One person will be on watch at all times, and they will all wear safety harnesses with tethers clipped to the boat at night and in heavy weather.

Ben is in charge of the first-aid kit because he is trained in emergency medical aid, and he adds all sorts of supplies to the kit, including several medications, along with a needle and thread for stitching. JP jokes that the boat now has its own pharmacy. But the "pharmacy" can't cure Ben's hangover after he and Rudy polish off four bottles of wine. The next day Rudy says the drinking served them well as "part of a team-building experience." Ben fires back, "Well, that may be, but I'm never drinking with a fuckin' Canuck again!"

The time spent working on the boat has been valuable for the three sailors to get to know one another before heading out to the open water. Rudy is glad for the few days of preparation; if he found anything of concern about his crewmates, he figured he could always back out of the voyage. He knows a transatlantic crossing has its risks, and he wants to feel extra comfortable with his partners. They will be in close quarters for several weeks. Rudy has a good feeling about both men. Ben is a knowledgeable sailor and a fun companion, and JP is soft-spoken, easygoing, and competent.

Departure is scheduled for May 1, 2007, but the men have to wait an extra day for some new batteries. This one-day delay will have significant consequences.

CHAPTER TWO

JEAN PIERRE

May 2, 2007

Before casting off at six-thirty in the morning, JP checks the marine weather forecast, but finds nothing out of the ordinary. Their destination is Gibraltar, but first they will land at the Azores for refueling. As they untie the lines, some friends from the marina come down to wave goodbye. JP then makes good on a promise. He will stop smoking now that the voyage has begun. To prove it, the short and slender captain with wispy gray hair takes his last pack of cigarettes, ceremonially holds them high in the air, and tosses them into the water—his new life as a nonsmoker begins at this moment. Rudy and Ben exchange glances; they hope their polite and relaxed captain doesn't turn into Ahab.

After doing some 360-degree turns to calibrate the new equipment, they slowly motor down the St. Johns River, going right through the heart of Jacksonville as the sun clears the eastern horizon. As they approach the first bridge, Rudy can't help but wonder if the mast—all sixty-one feet of it—will clear the underside, but JP assures him it will, and it does. Near the river's mouth, they stop at a marina to top off the diesel tanks and fill up jerricans with more fuel. During the refueling, Rudy announces, "I'll be right back. I'm going to make a last stop for food." He walks to a market and purchases three orders of fish and chips.

JP uses this opportunity to call his wife, Mayke (pronounced *My-keh*), a highly successful artist. They talk for a few moments, but JP wonders why Mayke is so mad at him for not calling earlier. She doesn't tell him the real reason: She has had an uneasy feeling—"the kind you get right where your navel is"—that this voyage will not end well.

Mayke knows her husband is a safety-conscious sailor and that the *Sean Seamour II* is more than capable of handling rough weather, but ever since she dropped JP at the airport a couple of weeks earlier, her apprehension has grown in intensity with each passing day. Sleep has been difficult, and her time painting in the studio has suffered. She just wants her conversation with JP to end before she blurts out her misgivings and puts a damper on JP's enthusiasm for the voyage.

When she hangs up the phone, Mayke tries to analyze her anxious mood, but she simply has no idea where it's coming from. If it's intuition, it seems totally illogical. But try as she might, she can't shake the feeling that the trip is doomed. She doesn't even try to return to the studio, knowing that anything she paints will be dark and foreboding.

When Rudy returns with the fish and chips, the men enjoy their lunch—their last meal from the outside world. Then they resume motoring, reaching the ocean at two p.m.

I'm finally doing it, thinks Rudy as he watches the shore disappear. *We're on our way.*

There's a slight breeze from the southwest, and the men are able to get their sails up, first heading in an easterly direction for about an hour and then sailing north-northeast. They are at the edge of the Gulf Stream, whose current will assist them on the first days of the journey. The balmy air allows the men to enjoy dinner in the cockpit, watching the sunset as they pull farther from land.

Later, while JP and Ben go to bed, Rudy stands watch to make sure they don't get too close to any other vessels. He is assisted by a radar detector that will sound an alarm if another vessel is in their vicinity. Rudy wears his safety harness with the tether clipped to a bed-eye or other firm object on the boat. This is a wise precaution to ensure that if someone accidentally falls overboard, the tether will keep him with the boat. Without the tether, a sailor who goes overboard at night has a slim chance of being found. There are few fates worse than swimming frantically and hollering in the darkness, trying to keep up with a boat whose stern lights are getting fainter and fainter as it sails into the night.

Rudy is glad he has the first watch; he's much too excited about starting the voyage to sleep, and he's already thinking ahead to tomorrow, his first full day at sea. Just before midnight, with a half-moon illuminating the water, Rudy has his first thrill of the trip. He's startled by a splash a couple of feet away from the boat. Peering at the ocean, he sees the outline of a dolphin come out of the water. There are perhaps twenty dolphins swimming along either side of the *Sean Seamour II,* occasionally breaking the surface with acrobatic leaps. Rudy watches, mesmerized. He has never seen dolphins at sea, and this pod seems to want to race the boat, just a few feet away from the awestruck Canadian. Grinning, Rudy feels a sense of well-being from contact with the natural world of the sea.

Looking from the radar screen back to the dolphins, Rudy expects the pod to veer away from the boat at any moment. Instead, they accompany the sailor for the next hour. Finally, at about one a.m., the dolphins leave, and Rudy checks a computer navigation screen that shows both the actual course of the sailboat and the course plotted in advance by JP. The vessel seems a bit off track. Rudy decides to wake JP and get his advice.

JP joins Rudy in the cockpit, and together they get the boat back on course. As they sail into the night, Rudy says, "Aren't you going back to bed?" JP shakes his head. "When I'm on the boat, I don't seem to require much sleep. It's a beautiful night, and I feel refreshed, so I'll stay up and enjoy it."

JP loves sailing so much, he doesn't want to miss any of it by sleeping. Like many die-hard sailors, he has had an unconventional life. Born in New York City, JP's father was French and his mother Belgian. They were not ready to raise a child and JP's father was abusive to both his son and wife. Because of the ill treatment, JP's mother fled her husband, abandoning her three-year-old son. It's a wonder JP survived the cruelties of his father. Neighbors heard him crying all the time and called social services when they realized he was left alone for hours on end in his father's New York City apartment.

Social services removed JP from the apartment and placed him in a foster home, which was little better than his lonely existence in the apartment. He was the youngest of several children there, and was ostracized by the older boys. But he was a resourceful child, and out of necessity he adapted, learning that he could survive by being alone and hiding when necessary. When he was six years old, his father somehow managed to regain custody of his child. JP went to live with him and his new wife, Betty. The resulting years were disastrous for young Jean Pierre. His stepmother, Betty, was a kind woman, but she, too, had to flee the cruelties of her husband, and once again JP, now ten years old, was alone with his physically abusive father. In an effort to get his second wife back, JP's father concocted a heinous plan, using JP as both pawn and victim. The father knew Betty loved the boy, and he surmised that if she realized JP was in trouble, she would return. In an unspeakable act of cruelty, his father intentionally dumped a pot of boiling water on his son, later claiming it was an accident. JP was brought to a hospital where a priest was ready to give the boy last rites. That was the last thing JP remembered. The scalding gave him second- and third-degree burns over most of his body, and for the next five weeks he was in a coma.

When JP emerged from the coma, he had to endure the latest burn treatment, which included being strapped to the bed. Nurses would have him lie for a couple of hours on his back and then rotate him onto his stomach so each side of his burned body would get air. Betty was a regular visitor, holding JP's hand, fighting back the tears whenever she looked in his sad eyes. He seemed to look right through her, a haunted gaze similar to that of soldiers returning from battle who have seen horrors few of us can imagine.

Somehow JP survived the trauma, and after several painful and lonely months in the hospital, he was well enough to be discharged. The "accident" accomplished his father's intended effect: Betty returned out of concern for the boy. She, too, was a victim of this manipulative and cunning madman.

Shortly after his recovery, Betty arranged for JP to be reunited with his biological mother, wanting to get him away from her husband. JP was shipped off yet again, this time to France, where his mother lived. In addition to being a better parent than his father, his mother lived in a place that was entirely different and exciting for the young boy, not just because it was a new country but because his mother lived by the sea.

The young boy who had endured so much cruelty found that the sea had a soothing effect. Saint-Tropez, on France's Mediterranean coast, opened JP's eyes to the marvels of the ocean, and he spent much of his free time prowling the seawalls while expectantly watching the fishing boats come and go from the port. He dreamed of hopping aboard one of the boats and traveling beyond the confines of the harbor, past the lighthouse, and out into the open ocean.

Soon the local fishermen noticed the quiet American boy watching them, and one kindly fisherman finally motioned for JP to come aboard his boat, explaining to the lad that if he arrived at the wharf early the next morning, he could ride with the fisherman as he performed his work. The next day JP reported for duty before dawn, and out to sea they went. After a couple of hours, when the net was hauled aboard, he helped the man sort his catch and perform a few other odd jobs. Although JP could speak little French, the old man and the young boy worked well together, and soon JP was a regular helper. The twosome would motor out in the boat before dawn and return with their catch in time for the morning market.

A year later, JP received his initiation to sailboats when he met an English sailor who was repairing his catamaran. JP watched and helped when he could as the man worked on his boat. The sailor told stories of his adventures at sea, which stimulated young JP's imagination and his growing desire to get his own sailboat. Through this Englishman, JP met other sailors and was soon crewing on centerboard sailboats.

When he was twelve years old, JP found a derelict sailboat that he rehabilitated as best he could, and soon he was sailing around the Gulf of Saint-Tropez, learning largely by trial and error. Over the next four years, the young sailor and his little boat would challenge the wind and seas far beyond the boat's designed purpose, first voyaging to Cap Camarat, then the isles of Levant, and finally out into the blue water of the open Mediterranean. It was on JP's solo trips that the idea percolated to someday sail across the Atlantic and later around the world.

JP's aspiration was further fueled when he read about the exploits of sixteen-year-old Robin Lee Graham, who set out to sail around the world in his twenty-four-foot sloop named *Dove*. *National*

Geographic published periodic articles of the young sailor's adventures as he sailed through the South Pacific, was demasted twice during storms, and met his future wife on the island of Fiji. Graham was not trying to set any records for speed; he was interested in exploring different ports of call, and this appealed to JP. It took Graham a little over four years to complete his journey, but nevertheless, when he finished in 1970, he became the youngest person to solo sail around the planet. Graham became JP's inspiration and hero.

JP thought the adventure of circumnavigating the world was the perfect challenge for him, and he vowed that someday he would set sail and not return until he had crossed the seven seas. Neither JP nor Graham minded being alone, but there was one big difference in their childhood. Graham had a loving father who taught his son to sail and celebrated his son's independent streak. But JP didn't let his past slow him down; he simply taught himself what he needed to know or asked questions of the fishermen and sailors of Saint-Tropez.

JP's dreams of blue-water sailing were put on hold when he was seventeen and attended landlocked Syracuse University in New York, followed by finding a job in Germany. The young man had an entrepreneurial spirit combined with a sharp mind that could intuitively solve problems. He also had a pair of hands that could make or fix just about anything. In 1978 he put those talents to use, starting his own business developing and marketing consumer products, including toys and household goods. Four years later, he sold the business but agreed to stay on for a couple of years in a senior management position. Although he was mostly away from the ocean, he read about the sea and went on day sails whenever possible, still dreaming of one day sailing around the world.

JP had married and fathered three children when new business opportunities prompted him and his family to move from Europe to the Washington, D.C., area. His heavy workload and frequent travel kept him not only from the sea but also from his family, and soon his marriage fractured, ending in divorce in 1995. During this period he purchased a country inn in Saignon, France, because his mother and stepfather needed work, and JP thought they could manage the business with his occasional oversight.

After the divorce, JP turned his attention back to the sea, often walking the harbors and boatyards, eying different models of sailboats. He viewed the vessels with a "champagne man's taste and a beer man's pocket," but finally found a compromise in a thirty-three-foot Beneteau Oceanis 321 that he christened the *Lou Pantai,* which roughly translates to "the Dream" in the old language of Provence. He moored the *Lou Pantai* at the Annapolis City Marina and lived aboard the boat during the coldest winter of his life, planning his blue-water getaway while shivering in the cabin. He consumed every sailing book he could find to help him prepare the vessel for a transatlantic crossing, and he purchased an EPIRB. JP was a loner by nature, and that cold winter, while living solo aboard his vessel, he felt exhilarated by the possibilities that stretched before him.

The next spring he sailed the Chesapeake Bay region, often traveling down to Smith and Tangier Islands. Those weekend trips taught him more about his vessel's capabilities, and he continued to upgrade the *Lou Pantai* for the voyage he planned across the Atlantic. With his analytical mind, he began to investigate every nook and cranny of the boat, seeing what improvements he could make, and pushing himself to understand how each and every piece of equipment functioned. One of his major changes was to remove the boat's batteries, which he did not feel would meet the needs of an ocean crossing. He replaced the batteries with eight six-volt golf cart batteries, rebuilding the hold to accommodate them. Using the same creativity that helped him start his own business, he installed a workbench, where he placed his cherished Zyliss aluminum-alloy multifunction bench tool. JP was an inventor at heart, and the bench tool allowed him to custom-make some of his own parts for the vessel. He also spent those first couple of years with the boat considering various problems that might crop up at sea and how to resolve them.

In 1996 JP began his long-awaited transatlantic trip. The first leg of the voyage took him to Cape Cod, Massachusetts, to visit his stepmother, Betty, and to finish provisioning the boat before the Atlantic crossing. He set sail from Annapolis on July 4, reaching the Cape a few days later. JP was ecstatic to be out on the open sea, feeling much like he did as a boy during that first trip on the fishing boat from Saint-Tropez.

JEAN PIERRE

Once moored at Cape Cod, JP had to wait for Hurricane Bertha to pass by, up the East Coast. When the storm had spun its way north of Massachusetts, he monitored the weather forecasts and decided he could set off safely for Europe. Betty went down to Harwich Port to see her stepson off with hugs, kisses, and more than a few tears. She waved goodbye as the *Lou Pantai* cleared the harbor, and then she drove down to Red River Beach, where she could see JP sailing eastward, fighting back tears until the boat became a speck on the horizon before disappearing from sight.

JP thought Hurricane Bertha was long gone, but the storm had a surprise for both meteorologists and the lone sailor. Four days into the voyage, while in the Gulf Stream, JP ran into building seas. Bertha, now downgraded, had not continued north after reaching the Maine coast, but instead had veered east-southeast and into the path of the *Lou Pantai*. The winds increased to over fifty knots, and the seas climbed to twenty-five feet. JP ran with the seas, and about midday he laid a drogue off the stern that provided better helm by slowing the boat when running down the following waves. Realizing he could not stay at the helm all night, he decided to deploy a sea anchor to keep the drift to a minimum. But as he prepared this equipment, an extreme wave spun the sailboat completely around, causing the slack in the line attached to the drogue to tangle in the propeller.

Battered by crashing waves, the *Lou Pantai* rolled so violently that JP had difficulty moving without being thrown to the deck. Water infiltrated the engine tank vents, and the boat lost power. The wind screamed through the rigging, fraying JP's nerves, making him feel like he was inside a screeching violin. Somehow he made it through the night without being injured, but during the next day and evening, the waves grew to thirty feet. JP's sole source of comfort was the knowledge that he had an EPIRB on board. Later that night, the seas became so chaotic that he considered activating the EPIRB, but he forced himself to hold back.

He was convinced the storm would eventually kill him, and during the desperate hours, he wrote a goodbye letter to each of his three children, telling them how much he loved them. When the notes were written, he sealed them in bottles and tossed them overboard.

Through the long and terrifying night, the wallowing *Lou Pantai* somehow remained afloat, and when dawn finally came, the winds abated a bit and JP knew the seas would follow. Later that day, when the waves became manageable, JP tied a line around his waist and entered the water with a mask and snorkel. Over a five-hour period, he worked on cutting the sea anchor line from the propeller and shaft. When the job was done, the bruised and exhausted sailor resumed heading eastward.

The rest of the voyage was without incident, and JP felt an enormous sense of gratitude and accomplishment. He had not only completed his transatlantic crossing but had survived the worst conditions that the ocean could throw at him. Or so he thought at the time.

CHAPTER THREE

RIDING THE GULF STREAM

May 3 is another fine day, and with a brisk breeze from the west, the *Sean Seamour II* is now traveling north-northeast, riding the current of the Gulf Stream. Rudy is surprised by the change in the ocean's color, from a greenish-gray hue to a brilliant aquamarine, and he marvels at the sun's ability to shine right through the top of small waves. He also notes that the ocean's temperature has climbed from the previous day's 73 degrees Fahrenheit to 78 today.

The warm waters of the Gulf Stream are a result of its origination in the Gulf of Mexico. Its current shoots through the fifty-mile-wide Florida Straits, passing between the tip of Florida and Cuba, sending the flow northward along Florida's eastern seaboard. Here the Gulf Stream is narrow, deep, and quick-moving, just like a high-speed river in a well-defined path, with only an occasional eddy forming at its margins. Approximately forty miles wide, a quarter mile deep, and traveling at a clip of four to five knots, this beginning section of the Gulf Stream carries a volume of water more than twenty-five times greater than all the rivers in the world combined. When it reaches Cape Hatteras, it curves to the northeast, losing a bit of its power as more warm-water eddies detach and re-form, while the Stream itself broadens and slows. Most of the warm-water eddies spin north out of the core of the Gulf Stream, rotating in a clockwise current, and some of these separate completely, spinning off on their own meandering path. Farther north, the Stream flows eastward, forming the North Atlantic Drift, slowly heading across the Atlantic and ultimately traveling past the British Isles. Although its temperatures are not as warm here as they are off Florida, the Gulf Stream still moderates the climate off Western

Europe and is said to be the reason why palm trees grow on the southern end of Great Britain.

Author William MacLeish points out that the moving mass of water in the Gulf Stream is not a highway just for sailboats but for fish and turtles as well, carrying them from the tropics to far-off shores such as New England. "Caribbean fish show up in the autumnal sea off Martha's Vineyard. Southern turtles ride past New England like sleeping commuters gone way beyond their stop. . . . It is clear that many organisms in the Stream are not there by choice and that many of those will eventually drift north to their deaths." MacLeish also points out that there are species that can live in the Sargasso Sea, the Gulf Stream, and even the cold waters to the north and west. "Some, the opportunists, seem to thrive where warm water and cold wrap around each other."

In the section of the Gulf Stream north of Cape Hatteras, its warm waters are in stark contrast to the cold ocean along the continental shelf to its north and west. On the Stream's eastern side is the Sargasso Sea, with its huge mats of free-floating brown seaweed called sargassum. Unlike the Gulf Stream, the Sargasso Sea is largely stationary and is known for a stable air mass that causes sailing vessels to become becalmed in its doldrums. Consequently, most sailors like those on the *Sean Seamour II,* who are traveling from the U.S. to Europe, avoid going directly through the Sargasso Sea and instead hitch a ride on the Stream and sail just north of Bermuda before heading due east.

The Gulf Stream presents its own set of challenges. Its waters warm the air directly above it, helping to produce a microclimate. Sailors can often see the location of this saltwater river long before they arrive. Low clouds may hover above the Gulf Stream due to rising warm air and water vapor. If the warm air collides with a cold front, violent thunderstorms erupt, with severe localized wind, rain, lightning, and even the occasional waterspout. Yet forecasting when these thunderstorms will occur is difficult, due to the quickness of their formation.

Even worse than the thunderstorms are existing weather systems that intensify above the Gulf Stream when they feed off the warm ocean below. Tropical storms passing over the Stream can explode into full-fledged hurricanes, and sailors are especially wary during the height of hurricane season, in late August and September. In addition, the Gulf Stream is not the place to be caught in a storm, due to the size of the waves that occur there. When winds come out of the northeast, they produce waves surging toward the southwest, and these waves become larger and steeper when they run into the Gulf Stream's current flowing in the opposite direction. Steep waves suggest breaking waves, and these avalanching combers can cause havoc to boats. Some sailors would rather face a swell twice as big as a cresting wave simply because the swell slides under the boat, while the breaking part of a wave can push the boat down its face and engulf it in the churning water. And if a wave spins a boat completely around so that it comes down the face of a wave bow-first, the ultimate disaster can occur. The vessel can "pitch-pole." This happens when the bow is buried in the trough and the stern is picked up by the surging sea and hurled over the bow, capsizing the boat in the process.

JP is aware of the advantages and potential dangers of voyaging along the Gulf Stream, which is yet another reason he chose the beginning of May to set sail. He knows he will be well beyond Bermuda by June 1, the start of hurricane season. Several other sailboats are also in the Gulf Stream, making their annual voyage from the Southern U.S. and Caribbean toward the cooler climates of ports from Maryland to Maine.

That afternoon Ben surprises his crew members with an English custom by serving them tea. A little later, dinner is prepared by Rudy (the men will take turns), and as on the previous day, they take advantage of the fine weather by eating in the open air of the cockpit, which is quite comfortable. It features a seat for the helmsman behind the wheel and cushioned benches for passengers. The hard dodger protects the front of the cockpit from spray. To the rear of the cockpit is a stainless steel arch, home to most of the *Sean Seamour II*'s passive and active sensors from radar to GPS and NAVTEX, as well as the wind generator used to produce electricity to sustain the electronic system aboard. Just beyond the arch is the canister that contains the six-person Zodiac Bombard offshore life raft. Two lifelines surround the entire perimeter of the boat. The interior of the boat is as comfortable as the cockpit, and elegant, with the gleaming cherrywood that JP selected for the cabin's trim. From the cockpit, there are three steps down the companionway that lead to the main salon. The chart table and communications center is to starboard, while on the port side is the dining table and wraparound settee. Just aft of the chart table is the galley on the starboard side, followed by the main cabin and the head (bathroom), boasting a bathtub to port.

As the men eat dinner, JP mentions that the latest weather report continues to call for favorable conditions. Rudy can't remember when he last felt so relaxed. No phone calls, no television, and no schedules. Even the sunset looks as stunning as any he's ever seen, with shades of pink, red, and orange shining over the dark sea below. A bit later, when it is completely dark, he sees his first phosphorescence. The strange light is caused by the chemical reactions in bioluminescent plankton. Because earlier mariners incorrectly thought the shimmering light was the mineral phosphorus, the term "phosphorescence" is sometimes used for the strange phenomenon of the glowing plankton. Its beauty is enhanced by the waves, moving the plankton and causing its light to be bright one minute and less so the next. Some sailors think the radiant light looks like millions of stars or an aurora borealis; others think it resembles the twinkling lights of a city seen from an airplane. Rudy just thinks it's beautiful.

The entire trip so far has been magical for Rudy: the dolphins, the changes provided by the Gulf Stream, and now the shimmering sea. Ben and JP have seen these marvels on their prior trips, but observing Rudy's astonishment makes them feel the wonder anew. The *Sean Seamour II* is sailing smartly, and in the distance they see the lights of a large ship passing by and the light from a nearby weather buoy.

As the men enjoy the night, Rudy asks JP how he came to own the *Sean Seamour II*. JP smiles and thinks, *Where to begin?* He explains that after he crossed the Atlantic in his first boat, the *Lou Pantai*, he devoted the next couple of years to actively managing his inn in France while increasing its size by six additional guest rooms. It was during this period that he met Mayke, and their relationship blossomed during trips on the *Lou Pantai*. They eventually replaced the *Lou Pantai* with the *Sean Seamour I,* soon to be followed by the larger

Sean Seamour II. JP had learned much on his earlier Atlantic crossing and felt the *Sean Seamour II*—a heavier boat with a center cockpit—would be ideal for his ultimate goal of circumnavigating the globe. The name of the last two vessels was chosen by Mayke and is a play on Jean Pierre's first name and his love of the sea: "sea" and *amour* (which means "love" in French).

In 2002 JP and Mayke decided to move the *Sean Seamour II* from France to the eastern seaboard of America, where they were considering settling down. The couple took the vessel on the first leg of the journey westward through the Mediterranean, then past the Canary Islands, continuing to Cape Verde. Because JP was needed back at the inn, he hired a charter captain to take the vessel the rest of the way to Florida. Later, when time allowed, the couple flew to Florida, where the vessel was moored in Tampa, and they took an extended sail, first voyaging southward through the Florida Keys, then northward through the Intercoastal Waterway to Chesapeake Bay.

On a different trip in 2003, they visited Oriental, North Carolina, and found a house they liked so much they made an offer on it. Mayke, however, was not a U.S. citizen, and to buy a house together would involve loads of paperwork, expense, and time. JP had a plan to solve the problem: They would marry. While Mayke was getting ready for a day of sailing, JP scouted around for a justice of the peace and found one at the Oriental Town Hall. Then he rushed back to Mayke, who was in the shower. "Hurry up and get dressed!" JP hollered. "Come on, we're getting married." Mayke liked the idea, and an hour later, in a brief ceremony at the town hall, the two made it official.

Although the house in Oriental was a dream come true, the couple was unable to sell the inn quickly, and as months dragged on without a buyer, they were forced to sell their newly bought North Carolina home.

When the inn finally did sell in 2006, JP and Mayke relocated to a remote hillside hamlet thirty miles north of Saint-Tropez, where they purchased another home. The only thing left to do was to sail the *Sean Seamour II* back across the Atlantic to its new home in a harbor not far from Saint-Tropez. Both JP and the vessel would then be back at the very place where he first fell in love with the sea.

JP wasn't sure what he would do next. He had not yet given up his dream of circumnavigation inspired by Robin Lee Graham's voyage on *Dove*. He felt a kinship with Graham, a fellow free spirit and nonconformist who wasn't afraid of hard work or risk. But Graham had done his voyage when he was quite young, and now JP was fifty-seven with a wife and a home that needed much work. He resolved to keep an open mind and let life take its course. Whether or not he made his around-the-world voyage, JP had finally found true happiness with Mayke in their hillside home, and for the first time in his life felt truly content.

CHAPTER FOUR

SPIRITS ARE HIGH

May 4 is another sunny day, but with little wind the crew of the *Sean Seamour II* relies on the boat's motor to propel them northward. JP senses a change in the weather pattern and carefully analyzes the latest updates but discerns nothing ominous. As the morning progresses into afternoon, the temperature climbs, and Rudy announces that he's going for a swim. Ben and JP look at him like he's lost his mind, but Rudy says he's serious. JP kills the engine, and the boat comes to a stop.

Rudy dives into the sea from a small platform at the stern of the boat. As he surfaces with water streaming off his gray beard, he shouts, "Come on in!"

JP and Ben smile and shake their heads. Rudy tries again: "The water is like a warm bath!" He's got a smile from ear to ear; it's clear he absolutely loves taking a swim so many miles out to sea.

Ben and JP stand on the deck scrutinizing their crewmate as he breaststrokes around the sailboat. He doesn't look cold. It's clear that Rudy is truly enjoying himself. JP glances at Ben and says, "What the heck, let's join him." Within a minute, the two men dive in and join their friend, invigorated by the water, which, while not quite "bath" temperature, is still pleasant enough.

None of the men express concern about sharks, though the Gulf Stream has its fair share, from migrating great whites to prowling makos that can grow to thirteen feet in length. The mako is the more aggressive of the two and can reach speeds up to thirty-five miles per hour. "Shark hunter" anglers have seen hooked makos leap out of the water almost twenty feet in the air, and more than one mako has then turned and attacked the boat where the anglers stand in disbelief.

Sharks can sense vibrations in the water from long distances, and on this calm day, the movement of the swimming men would be easy to detect. The sailors know there are sharks close to shore, as well as offshore, and 99 percent of the time they avoid humans. JP gives them little thought, because he has never been bothered by the predators of the sea in his many years of diving and snorkeling. Unlike JP, Graham had several encounters with sharks while diving, and he was not fond of the creatures. In his book *Dove,* Graham wrote that a shark bit off his taffrail log spinner (which measures distance traveled), which trailed behind the boat on twenty feet of line. Graham was none too pleased. "I happen to hate sharks," he wrote. "When the five-footer [that bit off his spinner] finned at my stern I shot him with my .22 pistol. The brute opened his mouth in surprise, showing teeth that looked like they could snap a telephone pole. He thrashed wildly with his tail and then slowly keeled over and sank." In another instance, Graham described how the natives on a South Pacific island showed real interest when he swam from the beach to his boat, *Dove*. Later, he learned that this was the area where the islanders threw their dead into the sea; they were watching Graham because they expected him to encounter a shark, and they wanted to see the battle!

Sharks are not the only large predators in the Gulf Stream. Yellow-fin tuna, mahimahi, and blue marlin all hunt there as part of the food chain that starts with plankton and progresses up through various sizes of bait fish and on to the bigger fish. Writers from Zane Grey to Ernest Hemingway have told tales of epic angling battles with large fish in the Gulf Stream, and that is what JP has in mind after his crew safely completes the swim.

After sunning himself for a few minutes on deck, JP goes below and comes back with a fishing rod and a gaudily colored lure that he trolls behind the vessel as he restarts the motor and begins steaming ahead. The afternoon passes quietly, and the fish don't bite, so the men decide to try their luck tomorrow.

May 5 begins as a quiet morning, and the *Sean Seamour II* continues northward under power rather than sails. JP works on equipment, Ben catches up on reading in his berth, and Rudy mans the cockpit, looking out over the endless expanse of calm blue ocean. The fishing rod is set in the rod holder, and its line trails far behind the boat. A small bell hangs near the tip of the rod so that if no one is paying attention and a fish strikes the lure, the men will hear the tinkling bell as the rod tip jerks toward the sea.

Around midday Rudy sees his first flying fish. He is astonished by just how far it can leap, using its wing-like pectoral fins to glide over the ocean's surface. The flying fish he watches covers well over seventy-five feet in a straight trajectory with little arch. They burst from the water using their tail to power them upward, and once airborne, they take advantage of updrafts at the leading edge of waves to cover great distances, usually to escape predators. Some schools have been clocked doing close to forty miles per hour and traveling more than a thousand feet at a height of twenty feet above the water.

In the afternoon Ben is on deck and hears the bell on the fishing rod ring. He springs up and grabs the rod, which is arched over at an almost ninety-degree angle. Something large has grabbed the lure, and Ben hollers to his crewmates that a fish is on.

Ben, Rudy, and JP take turns with the rod, cranking the reel, putting all their strength into bringing the catch closer to the boat. They have no idea what is on the other end; although the fish is fighting hard, it never jumps. Ben grabs a gaff and waits by the stern. Finally, after a twenty-minute fight, the three men get a good look at the fish. It's a mahimahi, and they whoop with joy, knowing what a fine-tasting fish it is.

Also known as the dolphin fish, mahimahi (Hawaiian for "strong strong") is a beautifully colored creature with an iridescent gold and blue body and a strange-looking head. Instead of the top of the head tapering gently toward the mouth as with most fish, the male mahimahi's head is rounded, and the female's head is almost flat. While most mahimahi average three to six pounds and a couple of feet long, they can grow as large as five feet.

The mahimahi JP is now fighting appears to be a big one, and he carefully guides it toward where Ben is crouched with the gaff. Ben reaches down, lets the point of the gaff get under the fish, and then yanks it up with both hands, and the prize is on the deck. The mahimahi is almost four feet and a solid twenty-five pounds: enough meat for dinner and many fillets for the freezer.

Before Ben and JP begin to fillet the fish on the stern deck, JP reminds Rudy to make sure all the portholes in his cabin are shut, as Rudy's berth is directly below where they will be cleaning the fish and washing the deck down. Rudy goes below and closes his hatches but somehow misses the one right over his bunk. Sure enough, when JP later pours buckets of seawater over the deck to wash off the fish blood, some of it goes right into the open porthole below. The men have a good laugh later when Rudy comes up from below, saying his cabin smells like fish.

That evening the sailors enjoy dinner on the open deck. JP normally operates a dry boat, but to celebrate the fresh mahimahi, he and Ben enjoy a cold beer. It's another evening in a warm paradise as the western sky turns shades of purple and pink.

JP stares toward the setting sun longer than the others and observes that the western edge of the Gulf Stream appears to be clouding up. After the meal, he downloads weather reports for the second time that day but again notes that the two low-pressure systems and the two high-pressure systems spread out over the western Atlantic are in about the same positions. The forecast does not call for any storms in their vicinity, so JP keeps the boat on the current course but a wary eye on the clouds to the west.

That night, during Rudy's watch, high, thin clouds occasionally block out the moon and stars, and the night is as black as obsidian. When a break in the clouds occurs, the stars seem to overflow from the opening, and Rudy feels as if he can almost reach out and grab one. Random thoughts flow through his mind like the drifting clouds above. He's glad he decided to retire early from his position as a vice president with his local teachers' federation, allowing time for this voyage. He thinks of his father and two friends who died before they had a chance to do the things they planned for retirement.

Next Rudy thinks of JP and what an unusual man he is, with so many skills. He recalls how JP almost had to cancel the trip because of an infection he suffered from hand surgery, and how, when the voyage was in doubt, JP offered to reimburse Rudy for all of the money he'd spent associated with the voyage, including his airline ticket and any gear. This gave Rudy a favorable impression of the captain before he even stepped on the boat, and when he watched JP meticulously repair gear—including a broken clock that he completely disassembled and reconstructed like a surgeon—he knew the man had a highly analytical and technical talent. It was a minor accident involving JP that really caught Rudy's attention. Just prior to setting sail, the two men were working on a piece of equipment. While JP held the gear, he instructed Rudy to give it a good whack with a hammer. Rudy missed the mark, and the hammer landed squarely on JP's thumb. The captain didn't even flinch. After apologizing, Rudy asked JP if he was impervious to pain, and JP said, "Real pain is when you are burned all over your body and the treatment involves rotating you from one side to the other." Later, JP told Rudy a bit more about his scalding, and about his difficult childhood.

Rudy thinks it a strange coincidence that he, too, suffered burns long ago. In Rudy's case, the injury was an accident that occurred just after his birth in Holland, when a hot-water bottle broke next to his back. The burn was so severe that his spinal cord was visible, and the doctors told his parents he would not recover. Although Rudy survived, his early years were almost as difficult as JP's, because his birth occurred during the Nazi occupation of Holland during the so-called hunger winter in World War II. It was an extremely difficult time for his family and the nation as a whole, as the Nazis plundered the country and food became scarce. Thousands starved and others were prisoners in their own land; many were shot on sight if they ventured out after dark.

Partly because of their arduous younger years and partly because they were close in age, the two men quickly bonded and often talked of their past—the good times and the bad. Both men had grown children, both had worked hard to assist them with college tuition, and both had been through a divorce. Now the two sailors finally had the time to enjoy their love of sailing without a tight time constraint. Ben was much younger, and still single, and he brought the perspective of a new generation whenever the three men talked, which enriched their discussions. With his subtle sense of humor, Ben kept the conversations from getting too serious and entertained the two older men with stories of his recent adventures in far-flung ports.

•   •   •

Later that night, when JP comes up to relieve Rudy of his watch, the captain says he thinks it prudent to adjust their course. The squall lines on the western edge of the Gulf Stream are moving east, and the latest weather report shows the two low-pressure systems moving a bit closer. JP explains that if heavy weather is to hit, he wants to be out of the Gulf Stream. They will exit the Stream by heading east. He wants to play it safe.

Near dawn, Ben enters the cockpit to relieve JP of watch. The skipper uses the break to download the latest weather information, which predicts that in the next few hours, the winds will reach twenty to thirty-five knots and come out of the north. JP shares the news with Ben, and the two sailors agree that the change in course is the right move. Ben jokes that Rudy might get his wish and be able to sail through a patch of rough weather.

The change in the weather does have one benefit: The men can get the sails up and move along at a good clip. Spirits are high, and the sailors enjoy a bracing ride that increases to seven knots. Even if the wind does reach thirty-five knots, both Ben and JP have sailed through far stronger, and they are exhilarated rather than fearful as the *Sean Seamour II* plows evenly through the still-calm ocean.

CHAPTER FIVE

THE GATHERING STORM

That same day at JP's hillside home in France, his wife, Mayke, begins her daily hike with her two dogs up to their mountaintop perch with tremendous views to the east. She and the dogs climb up a rough dirt road littered with rocks, past the ancient chestnut trees rising from enormous gnarled trunks, and finally into the high country of low shrubs where wild boars live. She passes a rocky cliff where JP removed the flattest stones to use in the columns of the gate by his vegetable garden. She wonders how he is faring on his voyage and how far up the Gulf Stream he might be. Since he left on the trip, her days have been agonizingly slow, and painting has been difficult. The subject of each of Mayke's paintings is never planned out—she lets her hands guide her, and images begin to take form. Her last painting was of a woman sitting alone, staring at an open door.

It takes her a bit longer than usual to reach the summit because she hasn't been sleeping well from being on edge, worrying about JP. These climbs to the hilltop usually relax her, but not today. When she reaches the mountaintop, she sits down and gazes across the hazy valley to the next ridge, over five miles away. After a few minutes, her heart starts racing and the landscape she is staring at is replaced by a vision. She sees the inside of a boat, dark except for a few dim and flickering lights glowing from various pieces of electronic equipment. The cabin is moving violently, first up and down and then yawing from side to side. Her heart beats faster. *What is this?* she asks herself, feeling alarmed and nauseated. Her eyes are open, and she is not asleep, not dreaming. Then, as suddenly as the vision came, it is gone, and before her are the green hills stretching off toward blue skies. With shaking hands, she lights a cigarette and wishes she could tell JP to abort the trip and sail to the closest port. She doesn't know there are no ports near the current position of the *Sean Seamour II*. The vessel is approximately 240 miles off Cape Hatteras, North Carolina, and 400 miles from Bermuda.

Across the ocean, JP is taking over the watch from Rudy, sitting alone in the cockpit of his boat, trying but failing to appreciate another sunrise. His thoughts are fixated on the latest weather report downloaded from the Internet, showing the low-pressure system to the north of the *Sean Seamour II* deepening and gathering strength, its pressure gradients becoming more compact. To the south, the other low-pressure system is moving in a northwesterly direction, slowly closing the gap. Forecasters are calling for winds to increase throughout the day and max out at thirty to thirty-five knots.

JP squints at the horizon and sees an aircraft carrier steaming off his starboard bow far in the distance, likely heading toward Norfolk, Virginia. He raises the carrier on the VHF radio, and the navy radio operator confirms that their latest weather report is the same as JP's: increasing wind with rain as the low-pressure system intensifies. JP thanks them and continues to sail east, away from both systems and the potential hazards of the Gulf Stream.

Later in the morning, Ben and Rudy are in the cockpit, thankful for the great speed they are making away from the Stream. The seas are four feet and choppy, but the *Sean Seamour II* slices through them at seven and a half knots. This is the kind of sailing Rudy had hoped for. The invigorating breeze, salt air, and steady progress of the boat make him feel completely alive.

At one p.m. the two men notice wispy yellow-brown clouds off to the north.

"What do you make of those clouds?" asks Rudy, keeping his eyes fixed northward.

"Rain is coming, and maybe a squall," answers Ben.

Rudy nods. "I don't think I've ever seen clouds that color. They're so menacing."

JP comes up from below, glances toward the stained clouds and says, "The winds are forecast to veer out of the north to northeast late in the day, and that's when they are supposed to really pick up. We're in for some rough weather, so let's prepare."

The three sailors discuss the approaching weather and decide they don't want to get caught with too much sail up. They begin reefing the sails but continue advancing toward the east and away from the Gulf Stream. JP gets the canvas sides with plastic windows and attaches them to the hard dodger on either side to form an enclosure in the cockpit. The day darkens ominously, as if the sky is in a surly mood that might swell into all-out anger at any moment.

As the winds increase, the men realize the canvas sides will be blown apart, so Ben and Rudy take down what JP just put up. The cushions on the foredeck, although secured with rails and zippers on all four sides, start to flap and are in danger of tearing away under the strain of the wind. Tethered to the safety line that runs the length of the boat along either side, JP crawls forward to secure the cushions. Although the boat is handling the seas well, it is being rocked and jolted. Ben, who is watching JP crawl along the exposed deck, shouts above the wind to Rudy, "This is crazy. He should just let them go." But JP, being quite attached to the *Sean Seamour II,* has no such thoughts. He saves the cushions and is soon back in the cockpit.

An hour later, the winds are howling at forty-five knots out of the north-northwest. Raindrops, propelled horizontally by the wind, lash at the three sailors. JP thinks, *This is not good. Nothing is going as planned. The weather is not as predicted.*

Even though they are almost fifty miles east of the Gulf Stream, it still influences the gray seas around them because they are at the edge of a large eddy that has extended outward from the Stream. The seas are chaotic and have grown to ten to fifteen feet. JP reefs the remaining sails and then raises a small portion of a storm jib. The progress of the *Sean Seamour II* has slowed considerably, and cold rain pours from the angry sky. All three men put on their safety harnesses and tether themselves to the boat. Rudy has long since stopped reveling in the boat's bracing ride and is becoming increasingly concerned about the wind, which seems to get stronger by the minute.

As the afternoon wears on with no letup from the storm, JP considers his options. His original plan to sail north of Bermuda later that night no longer looks feasible with the diminished headway.

Making a run to Norfolk is out of the question because they would have to cross the Gulf Stream, and besides, they are much too far out to sea to beat the storm to land. The storm is already happening.

JP checks the latest weather reports, but they are the same, forecasting maximum winds of thirty-five knots. *Well,* he thinks, *I learned from Hurricane Bertha to expect the unexpected.* And this is the unexpected: JP is soon clocking gusts of up to sixty knots that cause the *Sean Seamour II* to pitch and roll, which makes moving about increasingly difficult. He decides the best course of action is to reverse course and run with the system. Even with the anticipated wind shift out of the north-northwest to the north-northeast, he has plenty of sea room to run and still avoid the Gulf Stream. He also decides to lay his largest drogue off the stern and let the boat run bare poles with the seas. The drogue is a wise choice, since it acts as a drag on the boat, counteracting the wind and waves that push the boat forward. The drogue device looks like a parachute with holes on its side trailed at the end of a long line, and like a parachute it can be a lifesaver. Besides slowing the *Sean Seamour II,* it also helps stabilize the helm and keeps the boat perpendicular to the sea, with its stern into the wind rather than beam-on.

Ben and Rudy assist JP with the drogue, feeding the drogue line through the main winch on the port side. JP crawls to the stern of the vessel and guides it through the starboard stern cleat. Despite the heaving boat, JP has no trouble balancing while he works. For a fifty-seven-year-old man, he is nimble, and his motions are quick and efficient—almost catlike. Approximately three hundred feet of line is released, so that the drogue lies deep in the second following wave. The amount of line to let out is an inexact science: If you feed too much, slack can form, and the drogue loses traction, potentially allowing the boat to broach as it slides down a wave, but too little line will cause the boat to jerk violently. The men feel they have set out just the right amount, because the *Sean Seamour II* is riding the waves with much greater stability. To make sure the line doesn't chafe, JP adds layers of duct tape and nonsoluble grease around the section of line that will ride in the cleat. The worst thing would be for the line to suddenly snap: That would send the boat surging forward, whereupon it might surf down a wave sideways and slam into the trough where capsizing is a real possibility.

Ben has weathered storms at sea before, and he thinks this one is manageable, particularly now that the drogue is set. The wind seems to read his thoughts. A powerful gust blasts down on the men and pries Ben's tight-fitting wool cap right off his head, flinging it into the sea.

With the drogue in place, JP sets the autopilot. The three sailors go below, secure the companionway hatch behind them, and seal themselves in the belly of the boat. The *Sean Seamour II* is battened down, and all the men can do is wait for the winds to blow themselves out.

Daylight gives way to evening and the storm shows no signs of abating—in fact it is increasing in power. The snarling waves are twenty feet, and many are steep enough to break, filling the ocean with white water and streaks of foam. Each time a comber hits the hull, the entire boat shudders, and occasionally a larger wave slams the vessel with frightening power. More than one wave smacks so hard that Rudy likens it to being hit by a truck. *Good God,* he thinks, *that felt more like a solid object than liquid.* The three men glance at one another, but nobody says anything. They know they are in the grip of a major storm, and the only thing between them and the hungry ocean is the fiberglass hull of their vessel.

Around eight p.m., Rudy's curiosity gets the best of him. He takes a couple of steps up the companionway, partially slides back the hatch, and peers into the darkness. He is immediately greeted by stinging pellets of water that feel like tiny needles being stuck into his face. Cupping his hands around his eyes, he can see enormous black walls of water towering menacingly above the boat. It's a terrifying sight, and Rudy estimates that the waves are over thirty feet. The roar of the wind and crashing seas is deafening. He's seen and heard enough and ducks his head, seals the hatch, and climbs below, telling the others about the size of the waves.

Rudy sits at the navigation station, keeping one hand on the seat and the other on the bulkhead to steady himself as the boat's motion becomes more and more erratic. Ben is wedged in tight at the salon, but JP can't seem to sit still. He's fidgeting and constantly checking instruments, his brow lined with concern. He has stopped checking the bilge level, knowing that even after extra packing in the well and tightening of the rudder stock collar, some water is seeping in. His real concern is the mounting force of the storm. With waves this brutal and steep, the drogue is the lifeline of the boat.

Rudy checks the anemometer and can't believe his eyes. Whenever the boat rides up out of the trough, they are assaulted by seventy-to-eighty-knot winds, with frequent gusts of eighty-five. He turns toward the others and shouts, "We just had a gust of eighty-five!"

JP is stunned. He knew it was bad out there, but eighty-five knots is crazy. He didn't even know his anemometer could measure anything beyond eighty. The storm is exploding so fast, it is hard to believe.

Ben shakes his head and says, "Well, that's something to tell my mates back home."

JP doesn't say anything, though he can't help thinking this is 1996 all over again and he's being mauled by the tail end of downgraded Hurricane Bertha. Only this time he knows the storm is even worse. He hopes the *Sean Seamour II,* a larger boat than his *Lou Pantai,* can withstand the punishment. Bertha almost killed him, and he knows he's in for a long night. This time around, he feels the added pressure of responsibility for Ben and Rudy. He hopes his silence does not betray his anguish for the extra burden he carries. Whatever this freak storm is, JP has a hunch that it is just getting started.

The storm pounding the *Sean Seamour II* has other sailboats in its clutches as well. The *Flying Colours* and the *Illusion* are near the Gulf Stream, while closer to shore the *Seeker* is battling the enormous waves. All are caught off guard by the sudden ferocity of this quick-forming storm.

Meteorologists are also surprised by the storm's behavior. Unlike many low-pressure systems that travel from the tropics or Africa and then expand when they reach the Gulf Stream, this storm began at the Stream, in the same region where the *Sean Seamour II* is being battered. The two minor low-pressure systems that JP was tracking earlier in the day pulled together to form one super cell that deepened so rapidly that no meteorologist could have predicted its power.

Adding to the storm's surprising characteristics, it does not travel up the coast, as most do, but instead wobbles in place and then ever so slowly drifts to the southeast. A strong high-pressure system to the north has blocked its path, ensuring that its fury will have plenty of time to generate mammoth waves.

Meteorologists call such a storm a bombogenesis because of how abruptly it forms and explodes. They will later label this early stage of the storm as an extra-tropical cyclone that will evolve into subtropical storm Andrea. But the sailors caught in the storm know only that they are being lashed by hurricane-force winds, and it doesn't matter that the "official" start of hurricane season is three weeks away. And the worse part is that there is not a damn thing they can do about it except sit tight, keep vigilant, and wait.

CHAPTER SIX

A CHAOTIC BREW OF WATER
AND A TERRIFYING NIGHT

Besides the four sailboats caught in the storm, a massive cargo ship, the 955-foot *Paris Express,* is plowing through the rampaging seas approximately twenty-five miles offshore from Cape Hatteras, North Carolina. Able to steam at twenty-eight knots, the ship has much greater stability and power to weather the storm. The ship's size and muscle, however, are no match for the waves, and at ten p.m. the vessel lurches so suddenly that twenty containers go crashing overboard.

The *Seeker* is a sailboat a few miles west of the ship, and should it hit a wayward container, the boat will crack like a ripe melon and spill its passengers into the hungry ocean. Many boats likely have gone down from collisions with these massive steel objects, because an estimated two thousand containers, either twenty or forty feet long, are lost at sea each year, and some float for extended periods. A container can be buoyant when it goes overboard door-side first and its internal load lodges against the door, trapping the air inside. A passing boat's radar may not detect the container because usually only a small portion of the steel box breaks the water's surface. A container can float this way for years until corrosion allows the air inside the compartment to escape.

As if dodging a container isn't enough to worry about, small boats also risk being run over by the cargo ship. Cargo ships are so big that a crew may not even know they've struck a yacht, and the mammoth vessels steam on. Or worse, the ship's crew may hear the muffled sound of an impact, but doesn't slow down to investigate because they're on a tight time schedule and the captain might not want to know what he hit. More than once a large ship has been identified as the culprit due to a slash of paint on its bow that matches the color of the missing boat.

Maybe it's a good thing the crew of the *Seeker* is unaware that there is a container ship nearby that has spilled some of its load. The crew has enough to worry about from the storm without the added knowledge that a giant vessel is being tossed around by the seas like a toy. On board the thirty-five-foot sailboat are three members of the Dixon family: husband, wife, and daughter, all from Bermuda. The vessel is approximately ten miles off Cape Hatteras. Earlier, Captain Dixon wanted to enter Oregon Inlet for safety, but the confused and chaotic waves made it too rough, so he was forced to drop anchor a few miles out. Because of the extreme conditions, the captain thought it prudent to alert the Coast Guard of his position even though he was not requesting assistance. Once contact had been made, it was determined that the *Seeker*'s captain should give the Coast Guard hourly updates regarding their situation.

The position of the *Seeker* is not very far from the deadly Diamond Shoals. These sifting sandbars extend southeastward from the tip of Cape Hatteras on the Outer Banks of North Carolina, and countless boats have foundered and sunk here, earning it the name "Graveyard of the Atlantic." Charts that might have been accurate one month can be obsolete the next as some sandbars are swept away only to be replaced by new ones in an entirely different spot.

Besides the ever-changing shoals, this section of the Atlantic is particularly treacherous because it is where the western edge of the north-flowing Gulf Stream collides with the south-moving cold Labrador Current, causing a chaotic brew of roiling water. In days gone by, ships heading south would be aided by the Labrador Current on their journey, but upon reaching Cape Hatteras, these same ships would be forced into a narrow channel because of the proximity of the Gulf Stream, which moves in the opposite direction. One mistake in navigation or a sudden squall could push a ship off course and send it either too close to shore, or into the Diamond Shoals, which can extend up to fourteen miles offshore. Lighthouses, buoys, and even manned lightships were used to warn mariners of the dangers, but men and ships still went down. It's as if the ocean proclaimed the turbulent waters off Cape Hatteras as off-limits to humankind, and enforced this decree with the loss of a ship and its entire crew.

More recently, with better weather forecasting and improved navigation technology, the accident rate has declined. But when a boat like the *Seeker* is surprised by a storm, its position is extremely vulnerable—particularly in the dark—as it gets penned in by the Gulf Stream on one side and the Diamond Shoals on the other. The best thing to do would be to maintain its position and ride out the storm. Unfortunately, the sailboat's small motor is not strong enough to hold the vessel in place against the wind and waves pounding its hull. And so the decision to drop anchor is the only practical option left.

The Dixon family is in for a terrifying night, a night during which their very survival may depend on whether or not the anchor holds.

While the *Seeker* is near dangerous shoals, the *Sean Seamour II,* the *Flying Colours,* and the *Illusion* are all near the Gulf Stream and vulnerable to the huge waves being spit out into surrounding waters. To illustrate how exposed they are, consider the case of the *Norwegian Dawn* in April 2005. The cruise liner, at more than nine hundred feet long, was steaming through the Gulf Stream on its way to New York when it encountered stormy weather. Two waves, estimated to be at least seventy feet in height, slammed into the ship, breaking windows, flooding sixty-two passenger cabins, and panicking passengers. One of the waves put green water over the bridge at ten stories high, ripping two hot tubs loose from the steel deck they were bolted to. A passenger later described how he had been asleep when he heard a loud boom. He woke his family, and they raced to a reception area where they found other passengers, some with wet feet, huddled together in life jackets. A few of the passengers thought the ship was going down and were crying hysterically. The captain diverted the ship to Charleston, South Carolina, for repairs, and that was where many of the passengers disembarked, abruptly ending their vacation, too traumatized by the event to continue a voyage at sea. The shaken passengers instead boarded a train to take them to New York.

The captain of the cruise ship, who had over twenty years of experience, said that he'd never experienced anything like the waves that damaged the vessel, and he explained how no one could have predicted that such giant seas would materialize so fast. Passengers felt differently, and many of them filed lawsuits contending that such powerful waves are to be expected in the Gulf Stream during storms, and the captain should have positioned the boat far away. Other passengers contended that because the vessel was to be featured on the Donald Trump TV reality show *The Apprentice,* the captain was rushing to New York City to make it to the taping of the show. A class action suit was filed maintaining that the passengers were knowingly put in harm's way to meet a schedule. In an article published by the Associated Press and Local10.com, an attorney for the passengers, Brett Rivkind, said, "The passengers feared for their lives. They were out on the open seas. People started putting on life jackets, expecting the worst. They started calling their loved ones to say goodbye."

In June 2007 a jury returned a verdict in favor of the *Norwegian Dawn*. This followed a favorable finding from the National Transportation Safety Board, which called the incident "an unavoidable encounter with severe weather and heavy seas."

Maritime meteorologists and Gulf Stream experts Jenifer and Dane Clark are all too familiar with the havoc that the Stream can cause. They believe that extreme waves in the Gulf Stream are more common than previously thought, and they are not at all surprised that the *Norwegian Dawn* incident occurred before hurricane season. "Some of the most intense storms we've ever seen happened in April and May. And waves that come up suddenly and have not traveled a far distance [the fetch] over the open ocean can be deadly. When you have big waves with little fetch, they are really dangerous because the wave period is shorter, meaning they are close together. One potential problem is that as your bow comes down off one wave, the trough is so small that the bow doesn't have a chance to start riding up the next wave, but instead gets buried by green water. The *Norwegian Dawn* was fortunate that the captain had reduced speed prior to the accident, and really lucky that a third seventy-footer didn't follow the first two."

In the *Norwegian Dawn* lawsuit, the Clarks testified for the prosecution, explaining that informed mariners recognize that the environment in the Gulf Stream can be quite different from the surrounding ocean. "When the *Norwegian Dawn* entered the Stream, the waves increased from seventeen feet outside the Stream to forty feet in the Stream within a one-hour period."

Even during a period of relatively low wind speeds of fifteen to twenty-five knots, the Stream can be a hazard for small boats if those winds are opposing the currents. Waves of seven to twelve feet can be generated, with the possibility of an extreme wave of up to twenty-four feet. So while the captain of the *Norwegian Dawn* said that no one could have predicted those giant waves, he should have known that when you are in or near the Gulf Stream during high winds, the *potential* for a rogue wave is much greater than in other parts of the sea.

The Clarks watch weather patterns over the Gulf Stream and try to warn mariners when the conditions are ripe for sudden seas. "Extreme waves produced near the Gulf Stream are not like tsunamis," says Dane. "They often only have a short life span, with amplitude building before they dissipate. But in that short life, they can be deadly."

During the evening hours of May 6 at the Coast Guard Air Station in Elizabeth City, North Carolina, the men and women on duty are well aware that a storm is building at sea. The Coast Guard knows the *Seeker* is trying to ride out the storm beyond Diamond Shoals, and they are anxiously awaiting each hourly update. The search and rescue center has a hunch there are more sailboats farther out at sea, but at this time they have not received any messages from the *Sean Seamour II,* the *Illusion,* or the *Flying Colours.* Those boats are beyond radio contact and, so far, are performing as well as can be expected and are not in emergency situations that would cause them to activate their EPIRBs.

Earlier that evening a Coast Guard C-130 plane had been dispatched as a safety measure to broadcast radio warnings about the storm to any vessels that could hear their message. Upon the plane's return flight to the air station, the pilots recognized that the cross winds were beyond the safe limit for landing on the station's only strip long enough to handle the large plane. The aircraft commander decided to fly north to the airport in Norfolk, Virginia, and land there. The plane was immediately refueled, and a new crew drove up from Elizabeth City to relieve the crew who landed. The new crew checked in to a hotel for a night's sleep, figuring there was an outside possibility that they would be instructed to launch the next day, should a vessel find itself in trouble.

The call will come much sooner than expected.

CHAPTER SEVEN

HELP IS GREATLY NEEDED

As the hour approaches midnight, the average wave size has increased to an incredible fifty feet, and the *Sean Seamour II* is carried up the face of each swell until it teeters at the very top and slips down the back side. Occasionally, a wave crests and breaks so that as the boat begins to rise, the comber cascades directly on it, jarring the men's bodies and their nerves as the sailboat takes the blow. Breaking seas mean steep seas, which alarms the men. They all know that one wave can engulf the boat and just about anything can happen. The vessel might be knocked on its side until it rights itself in the trough, or it could be knocked down and continue to roll 180 degrees in a complete capsizing. An even worse, but very real, scenario is if the drogue fails or is snapped free, the vessel could surf down an especially steep wave so fast that the bow will be buried in the trough and the stern picked up by the wave and pitched directly over the bow. This pitch-poling is so violent that some sailboats capsized in this manner suffer severe structural damage and never recover, as hundreds of gallons of water flood the interior. Should the sailboat stay in one piece, the passengers would likely be severely injured.

Ben is aware of these possibilities, and as he hears the occasional breaking seas outside the hull, he knows these fifty-foot mountains are pushing the limits of the *Sean Seamour II*. He has always known that blue-water sailing has its share of risks, and should he sail for a lifetime, he figured he'd eventually encounter danger. He just didn't expect it to come so soon in his sailing career. Then again, he thinks of JP and realizes that the captain has encountered extreme conditions on both of his attempted transatlantic crossings. It's really a roll of the dice as to when a sudden storm can form.

HELP IS GREATLY NEEDED

Rudy's luck is even worse—here he is, on his very first sailboat voyage on the ocean, and he's in the maw of a monster storm. He's not dwelling on his misfortune but instead is listening to the chaos outside. When the vessel takes a direct hit from a wave, the boat groans and Rudy feels it vibrate at the top of the comber, where the shrieking wind and churning water can fully attack the *Sean Seamour II*. He breathes a sigh of relief when the surging water passes and the vessel is in the eerie silence of the trough. Then the next wave comes, and the same terrible sensations begin again. The analogy to being on a roller coaster is an accurate one, particularly when the coaster approaches the top of the incline, where it always slows before plunging down, picking up speed all the while. It's that sense of hesitation and then of free fall, if only for a split second, that is so unnerving.

The waves are probing and jabbing the boat for weakness, ready to pounce if it should find any. Rudy can't help but think that the *Sean Seamour II* is in the hands of a raging giant who is shaking and then punching the boat, trying to get inside. Every now and then the sea—the giant—seems to relax a bit, as if gathering strength for the next onslaught. When a set of smaller waves slides under the boat, Rudy knows it's the briefest of lulls, to be followed by a renewed strike that seems more vicious and powerful than before.

Rudy is exhausted by the cumulative effect of the lurching boat, the loud thuds on the hull, and of not knowing how much worse it will get. The uncertainty of what lies ahead makes it near impossible to relax. The waiting seems interminable, and he feels like he's been in the storm for two days rather than a few hours.

It's just after midnight, and May 6—one of the longest days of the three men's lives—is behind them. They wonder what May 7 will bring. Rudy eats a couple of granola bars for energy, offering some to JP and Ben, then decides that if he doesn't at least try to get some rest, he will be too fatigued to be useful when the storm abates. His nerves are frayed, and his muscles tired and cramped from sitting by the chart table and tensing up each time a wave pounds the hull. He suspects the two other men feel the same, even though no one has said a word for the last half hour.

"There's nothing we can do sitting here," says Rudy to his mates.

"Why don't a couple of us try to rest and then relieve whoever is still up."

JP says there's no way he can lie down, but he encourages Ben and Rudy to do so. Ben thinks, *This is worse than being held captive. We can't fight back in any way.* He's right, there are no more precautions they can take, and even if they think of one, it's too dangerous to go topside. It's all up to the boat. Every screw, rivet, line, seam, porthole, and the rest of what makes up a sailboat has to hold under the assault of the seas.

Ben lies down on the port settee where he has been sitting, folds his arms across his chest, and closes his eyes. Rudy lurches to the rear cabin and lies down on the bed. He hears the autopilot gears making a high-pitched whine from the strain of the seas. The noise is awful, and he can only imagine what's happening outside the boat. He goes back and tells JP about the autopilot, saying something will break if it's allowed to continue.

JP has also heard the autopilot overcompensating. He shuts it off, then takes a seat at the chart table to make manual helm adjustments. The wind has veered farther out of the north-northeast, and he senses the seas are changing pattern, so he recalibrates the computer for a resetting of the rudder response, finally finding the right yet precarious balance. He wonders what the topside of his boat looks like and assumes there will be plenty to fix the next day. It is now approximately one a.m.

The series of waves slamming the boat continues for a few more minutes, and suddenly there is a thunderous boom. In that second Rudy goes from resting in his bed to being airborne, hurled across his cabin and into the bulkhead, hurting his back. In the salon, Ben, too, is thrown in the air, traveling from the port side of the settee toward the chart table where JP is. To JP, it seems as if time has transitioned into slow motion. He can see Ben's arms and legs flailing, coming sideways through the air. JP instinctively raises his hands to protect himself, and in the next split second, Ben barrels into him. One of JP's hands makes contact with the back of Ben's head, and the other pushes his shoulders, deflecting Ben ever so slightly so that the two bodies avoid a bone-breaking collision. Ben is turned so that his back and buttocks hit the bulkhead where the TV is mounted; it shatters in a spray of glass and plastic.

HELP IS GREATLY NEEDED

All this happens in the first second of the furious impact of a rogue wave. In the next second the damage continues, sending the *Sean Seamour II* careening over on its starboard side. Objects not bolted down are hurled through the boat like missiles, and canned soft drinks burst like rockets, spraying in all directions. Almost as abruptly as the vessel was knocked down, she springs back up, and the loose objects roll to the opposite side of the cabin.

The men don't know it but the force of the wave was so great that it has snapped their drogue. There is nothing to slow the boat as the angry seas have their way with it.

Rudy and JP half walk, half crawl to Ben and help him up. He is bruised from being launched through the air, but he insists he is okay. JP's gaze sweeps through the galley and salon. He notes that while it is in shambles, there doesn't seem to be any seawater pouring in.

"What happened?" shouts Rudy. So much adrenaline is going through him that he forgets about the pain in his back.

"It was a knockdown!" hollers JP. "I've got to check the deck, got to see how bad things are!" He doesn't say that he thinks the boat totally capsized, rolling a complete 180 degrees.

JP is dressed in his yellow foul-weather gear and has on an un-inflated yellow life jacket that is part of his safety harness. Ben and Rudy are dressed the same way, except Ben's foul-weather gear is red.

JP climbs the companionway, pausing for a second at the top. *Think everything through. Nothing rash.* Carefully, he slides back the hatch. Pellets of spray pepper his face and sting his eyes. The volume from the wind roaring and the waves crashing sends a jolt of fear and adrenaline down his spine. Amazingly, the deck light is shining, and he can see that the mast is intact. Then his eyes widen as if he's been slapped in the face by an unseen hand. He realizes the entire hard-top dodger is gone. The older EPIRB from his previous vessel was mounted on its cradle and attached to the dodger, and of course that has been swept away as well. It does not have a hydrostatic release, so he assumes it sank with the heavy fiberglass dodger before it had a chance to transmit. The upper part of the helm pulpit has cracked off as well. Turning aft, he is surprised to see that not only is the arch in place but the wind generator is still attached and whirling away. He squints in the gloom farther aft and notices a wonderful sight. The container with the life raft in it is firmly secured to the vessel.

A wave breaks over the stern, soaking JP and sending water cascading down the companionway. There is nothing more he can do, so he ducks down and seals the hatch. A million thoughts are racing through his mind. *We've had a capsizing, and we are hundreds of miles from help. We likely have structural damage. I'm responsible for the safety of Ben and Rudy. What will happen if an even bigger wave hits the boat?* He realizes there is a good chance the vessel will be so damaged that it won't right itself, or if it does, it will still eventually sink. Even if the boat stays afloat and survives the storm, he reckons the damage will be such that the vessel will be adrift and in peril.

Ben and Rudy are staring at JP, waiting for him to speak. "The hard dodger is gone, and part of the pulpit. I don't know what other damage there is, but we have the life raft. We're going to need help no matter what happens, so I'm activating the GPIRB. Once they get the signal, the Coast Guard will get the info about the boat and call us on the Iridium satellite phone, and we can let them know what's happening."

JP figures that if the phone won't work, at least the Coast Guard will know there is a boat in trouble and can follow its location as it drifts. He is certain the Coast Guard knows about the hurricane-force winds, and he concludes that the conditions will prohibit any rescue by helicopter. *But at least they'll know where we are and will come as soon as they can.* And help is greatly needed. JP can sense that the vessel is not as stable as before and is taking more broadside hits, and he knows there is likely more damage than he could see when topside.

Rudy and Ben agree with the decision to set off the GPIRB. Ben has been in a storm during a previous transatlantic crossing, but nothing like this, and no knockdown. Hearing about the damage topside only confirms his feeling that the storm is overwhelming the boat's equipment. *At some point soon,* he thinks, *we've got a good chance of getting hit by another monster wave, and then it may be too late to call for help.*

Rudy is not only worried about the vessel, he's concerned that one of the crew may be injured. *It's a miracle no one is seriously hurt from being thrown across the boat. We need help. And we also need a little luck. We've got to make it to daylight. Everything will be better then.*

JP activates the GPIRB, and its small strobe light blinks as does the light that indicates the unit is transmitting. There is relief on the *Sean Seamour II*. Someone out there will know that there are three souls in distress.

Although the nearest Coast Guard base is hundreds of miles away, there may be ships in the area. The Amver program (automated mutual-assistance vessel rescue system) is often the best hope for a vessel like the *Sean Seamour II*. Established in 1958 and sponsored by the U.S. Coast Guard, Amver consists of ships, regardless of nation or flag, that have voluntarily enrolled in the program to help another vessel in the event of an emergency. Over nineteen thousand vessels participate, and whenever one of those ships is at sea, its location is tracked by a computer-based ship reporting system. Search and rescue authorities worldwide can then use the information to assist persons in danger at sea by diverting an Amver ship near the emergency location to go to the aid of those in need. When those in distress are far off the coast of the United States, an Amver vessel can reach the accident scene faster than the Coast Guard, and that can mean the difference between life and death.

In a storm as severe as the one hammering the *Sean Seamour II,* an Amver vessel, a Coast Guard vessel, or a Coast Guard aircraft will have an exceptionally difficult time coming to the aid of the sailboat. The waves are so big that the rescue ship will be put in jeopardy, and the winds so high that the same danger will await any aircraft. Making matters worse, it is nighttime, and the sailboat is slowly being torn apart.

The knockdown of a vessel by a wave is a larger version of a beachgoer being hit in the surf by a wave that happens to break exactly where the person is standing. It's almost impossible to stay upright when the full force of the wave collapses on you. With the *Sean Seamour II,* the boat has stayed upright for several hours, despite being walloped by waves that grew to fifty feet, with the occasional fifty-five-footer in the mix. Incredibly, these waves are bigger than the vessel, and it's a testimony to its construction that it rode on through the night as long as it did. For the most part, the waves slid underneath the boat. The loud thuds—the sound of water impacting against the hull—were the waves with crests that slammed against the vessel, staggering it until the wave continued its onward slide beneath the vessel. The wave that knocked the boat down was a bit different. It was likely sixty feet in height. As the comber lifted the *Sean Seamour II* out of the trough, it, too, began its slide beneath the keel. But the wave was so large, so steep, it could not support itself and probably started breaking halfway up its face, with the full force of the water not just slamming the hull but engulfing it. Like the beachgoer in heavy surf, the *Sean Seamour II* didn't stand a chance. The initial impact—the kinetic force of it—is what sent Ben and Rudy flying and then pushed the vessel down the face of the wave, where the following surge completed the capsizing.

The design of the sailboat, particularly its lack of large windows, was one reason the knockdown was not more catastrophic. In count-less Coast Guard marine casualty reports, the trouble on either a sailboat or a powerboat starts with a window or porthole. These struc-tures, even though most are made of Plexiglas, are usually the weakest points on a vessel. Windows slanted by the deck near the bow, rather than on the sides of the boat, are the most vulnerable in a storm; there, breaking waves plunge directly down on the vessel. The sheer force and weight of the wave—just one cubic yard of water weighs nearly a ton—dropping on a window will either break the window or loosen its mounting, making the next wave more likely to shatter it completely. Storm shutters can reinforce the window, but they must be installed before the trouble begins.

Once a window has been breached and water floods the boat, suc-ceeding waves will carry more water inside. Then the fight begins. Bilge pumps may become clogged with debris and shut down or be unable to keep up with the water. Crew members frantically bail with buckets, pots, pans, or whatever they can find, and they must dump that water out the broken window or out the companionway hatch, neither of which is a good option in a storm.

The window may not be the sole reason a boat goes down, but it is the first major problem that leads to more issues, the cumula-tive effects of which will doom the boat. The vessel can lose power from water shutting down the engine. On most powerboats, this is especially bad, since without the heavy keel of a sailboat, a powerboat broadside to huge seas will capsize, and unlike a sailboat, it will not right itself. But even a sailboat can be further crippled by loss of all power and having water short out emergency power batteries. Radio power will be lost, and interior and exterior lights and pumps will all shut down. All because of one vulnerable window or porthole.

The three men on the *Sean Seamour II* don't have any shattered windows to worry about—yet. Their focus is on the storm, whose magnitude was predicted by no one. They simply can't believe it is still raging, and they are trying not to dwell on whether or not it has peaked. If the last rogue wave had been a few feet larger, they know they may not have survived. And with the drogue severed from the vessel, it is mostly riding the waves beam-on, and occasionally surfing down some liquid cliffs at unchecked speeds.

PART II

CHAPTER EIGHT

MULTIPLE MAYDAYS – THE SAR COMMAND CENTER

Although it's the graveyard shift, Search and Rescue (SAR) Coordinator Brian Avelsgard is wide awake and busy at the Command Center in Portsmouth, Virginia. There are two other coordinators working alongside him, and they have also called their captain, David McBride, at home and woken him up to keep him apprised of the rapidly changing situation. Each of these coordinators has a computer with a dual monitor, a couple of phones, and an assortment of emergency procedure manuals for different scenarios. The computers are used for rescue planning. Coordinators can input the type of vessel (particularly the amount of freeboard exposed to the wind), the estimated flight time for a C-130 plane to reach the boat in distress, and current on-scene weather. The computer then assists the coordinator in determining where the vessel may have drifted by the time the aircraft arrives.

The SAR team is well aware that the low-pressure system has grown to a powerful storm centered approximately two hundred miles out to sea off the coast of the Carolinas. The prior evening, when the storm's leading edge first impacted the inshore waters, the coordinators worked a case involving three fishermen on an eighteen-foot powerboat. The captain of the vessel had radioed the Coast Guard at eight p.m., explaining that he and his friends were trapped in a salt marsh due to wind and waves overpowering the boat. Brian Avelsgard dispatched a small Coast Guard utility boat to rescue the crew, but the rescue attempt had to be aborted because the water in the marsh was not deep enough for the utility boat. The only way to get the men off the vessel was by helicopter, so one was dispatched at nine p.m. The rescue swimmer faced an unusual challenge. Instead of being dropped into the ocean, he was lowered into three feet of water with a mud bottom and performed the rescue while standing up. All three fishermen were hoisted up without incident.

Although the rescue sounds like a simple one, Avelsgard was relieved when it was over. Any time he sends a helicopter up at night, he knows the challenges to the crew are doubled. Now he must be cognizant of the fact that the helicopter crew has used up some of their flying hours. Crews have "bag limits," or maximum flight times that must be monitored to make sure they have some rest before logging too many hours. Exhaustion is as dangerous to flight personnel as weather conditions.

Now, at approximately two a.m., Avelsgard is keeping track of the sailing vessel *Seeker,* which is dragging anchor off Diamond Shoals. He has been in communication with Coast Guard Station Oregon Inlet, whose radio operator is in contact with the sailboat captain. They are hoping that the boat can remain in deep water until daybreak, when a rescue won't be as dangerous. The captain agrees that he is not in a Mayday situation and that he will keep the Coast Guard advised of his situation with periodic updates.

Suddenly, an EPIRB distress notification flashes on the SAR Center's designated computer screen. It is not from the *Seeker* but for a vessel named the *Lou Pantai.* Coordinator Avelsgard has no way of knowing that this is the name of JP's earlier boat, indicating that the signal came from JP's backup EPIRB. It washed off the *Sean Seamour II* during its knockdown and came free of the hardtop dodger so that it floated on the ocean and transmitted. (This is a minor miracle, because it does not have a hydrostatic release mechanism to free it from its cradle, so it should have sunk with the hardtop dodger.) At this point there is no location associated with the beacon. Avelsgard will have to wait for another satellite to pass before he can get a fix, and this length of time can vary widely from case to case. In the meantime, Avelsgard reviews the telephone contacts that the owner of the EPIRB listed when the device was first registered. By making these calls, the SAR Center can gather a wealth of preliminary information. First and foremost, coordinators hope they can talk to the captain of the vessel so they can find out if the EPIRB is a false alarm or truly a distress signal.

False alarms from EPIRBs are a major problem for SAR coordinators. Sometimes the EPIRB starts transmitting when it is undergoing a periodic checkup or when new batteries are installed. In other cases, a water-activated EPIRB is knocked off a boat and sends a signal, or it falls on deck and is activated before the crew can turn it off. If the crew is not in radio range, they have no way to tell the Coast Guard it is a false alarm. Occasionally, a boat owner buys an EPIRB and, incredibly, doesn't bother to complete the registration process. These signals are especially frustrating to the Coast Guard. If an unregistered EPIRB goes off, it might be a real emergency, but the Coast Guard will have nothing to work with if the first alert is from an undisclosed location due to poor satellite reception. Because the unit wasn't registered, the Coast Guard has no list of telephone numbers to call and start gathering information about the vessel and where it might be in its voyage. Anyone on a boat in distress without a registered EPIRB had better hope and pray that a subsequent satellite pass will give the SAR team an exact location. Otherwise the Coast Guard just knows that somewhere, anywhere, a boat's EPIRB is going off.

Captain McBride cites one last example why it's so important for the SAR coordinator to gather as much information as possible before sending a C-130 or helicopter crew into a dangerous storm. "Every now and then a captain of a vessel will activate the EPIRB thinking they are in real danger. Then an hour later, something changes—maybe they regain engine power, or maybe the waves abate a bit—and the vessel moves on. By the time our rescue crew arrives on-scene, the boat is gone, but our aircraft stays out in the storm searching for the vessel or people in the water."

While Avelsgard is dialing the number for the first contact associated with the *Lou Pantai,* yet another distress signal comes in. This one is from a GPIRB registered to a boat named the *Cold Duck*. A fixed location is given at approximately 225 nautical miles southeast of Elizabeth City, North Carolina, on the eastern side of the Gulf Stream near the center of the storm. One of the coordinators starts to call the *Cold Duck*'s contacts, starting with the home telephone number of the boat's captain, located in Alabama. The coordinator expects the captain's wife or a family member to answer and confirm that the vessel is out on the Atlantic and that the distress signal must be for real. Instead, the captain himself answers and says he is at home in bed. He explains that his boat is safely moored at a harbor on the Alabama coast and that the GPIRB must be malfunctioning or that someone tampered with it. The coordinator asks him to go down to the boat and disable the GPIRB so they don't get any more signals, especially since they are in the middle of coordinating two potential rescues during a storm.

What no one knows is that the identification number for the *Cold Duck*'s GPIRB is the same as the number assigned to the GPIRB that JP bought for the *Sean Seamour II*. The IDs are designated by the manufacturer, and it's up to the GPIRB's owner to fill out the forms that go to the National Oceanic and Atmospheric Administration (NOAA). Both JP and the *Cold Duck* owner did so correctly. JP's GPIRB was the older of the two, so he was the first one to send his information in. Months later, when the *Cold Duck* owner did the same thing, NOAA's clerical process showed that the same ID number had been registered earlier. The NOAA operator overrode JP's earlier registration, because each beacon is required to have a unique ID. The operator assumed that there was only one GPIRB, and it had been sold by the owner of the *Sean Seamour II* to the owner of the *Cold Duck,* so the registration for the *Cold Duck* became the active one. The whole GPIRB issue could have been catastrophic if JP had not kept the older EPIRB.

When an EPIRB is activated, a satellite detects the signal and relays the information to a NOAA group called Mission Control, located in Maryland. The operators at Mission Control decode the satellite information and convert it to longitude and latitude to determine which Coast Guard SAR Center is closest to the accident scene. The location fix, along with the identity of the vessel in distress, is passed to the proper SAR Center on a dedicated communication link via computer. This is how Brian Avelsgard was notified of the *Lou Pantai* EPIRB, followed by the *Cold Duck* GPIRB. Brian and his fellow SAR coordinators are focused on the *Lou Pantai* EPIRB (the one that fell off the *Sean Seamour II*), and just as he begins to call the first contact, a satellite gets a fix on the vessel and Mission Control relays the position: 225 nautical miles southeast of

Elizabeth City. Before Avelsgard can process that this is the same position as the *Cold Duck*'s—which they thought was from a malfunctioning GPIRB—yet another EPIRB signal is detected. This one is from the *Flying Colours,* though no location is fixed. "We got another one!" shouts Avelsgard.

Avelsgard and McBride don't need a location to know that the *Flying Colours* is likely off the coast of the Carolinas, where the storm must be exploding with more intensity than forecast. From Avelsgard's perspective, all hell seems to be breaking loose out at sea. He's had three emergency beacons go off in the last hour, and another vessel, the *Seeker,* is in trouble. The SAR coordinators know they are in for a hectic night, and each person digs in and begins the tasks associated with saving lives.

One of the coordinators alerts the Coast Guard C-130 captain on duty that they have an EPIRB hit with a fixed location and that he and his crew should prepare the plane and go to the scene. This advance work will take a bit longer than normal because the C-130 that's ready for the mission is the one that landed at the civilian airport in Norfolk rather than the Coast Guard air station at Elizabeth City. The direction of the strong wind gusts at Elizabeth City is the same as the previous evening, so the safer runway is the one at Norfolk. The C-130 crew, staying at a hotel in Norfolk, hop in a van and race to the airport.

SAR coordinators activate the Amver program, but there are no ships near the coordinates from the EPIRB associated with the *Lou Pantai*. The closest Coast Guard cutter, the *Tampa,* is diverted from fisheries patrol off the coast of New Jersey to the distress scene of the *Lou Pantai* and the *Flying Colours*. It will not be an easy mission in such brutal, rampaging seas. They don't expect to arrive for twenty-seven bruising hours. The captain of the *Tampa,* Steven A. Banks, likens the beating they take to being inside a 270-foot-long washing machine in the agitation cycle. Trying to operate in that wild motion takes its toll on the crew; many have sustained cuts and bruises as they brace themselves at their various stations. All the Coasties are focused on reaching the distress area as quickly as humanly possible, knowing that sailors might literally be barely hanging on to life. On board the *Tampa* is sophisticated radar supplemented by "Big Eye" binoculars; both are just the kind of equipment able to find a cap-sized boat or life raft.

The telephone calls to the contacts for the *Lou Pantai* are not going well. First JP's son and daughter are contacted, and both tell the Coast Guard that their father sold that boat years ago. They explain that their father has a newer boat, the *Sean Seamour II,* but they don't know if it is still in port outside Jacksonville, Florida, or if JP is even on it. Now the coordinators are really confused. Avelsgard thinks, *This is bizarre. We have one emergency beacon to a vessel called the* Cold Duck *which is in port in Alabama, another to a vessel called the* Lou Pantai *that's registered to a captain who sold it years ago.* Then he realizes both emergency beacons are transmitting from the same location in the Atlantic, near the storm's center. He is certain a boat is in trouble there, and he's glad he alerted the C-130 crew to get ready to launch. He continues down the contacts for the *Lou Pantai* until he reaches a woman named Betty de Lutz, on Cape Cod.

Betty—Jean Pierre's stepmother—is woken from a sound sleep by the ringing of the telephone. "Hello," she answers groggily.

"This is the U.S. Coast Guard calling. Is your son, Jean Pierre de Lutz, on the ocean?"

"Yes," she answers with trepidation.

"We have an emergency beacon registered to him going off. Do you know the name of his boat?"

"I'm not sure."

"Is it the *Lou Pantai*?"

"Well, that was the name of his old boat, but he sold it. He now has a larger boat, but I'm not sure of its name. But if you have an emergency signal, it must be from him."

Avelsgard tells Betty they are preparing to launch a C-130 plane to go to the boat. "We will call you back soon and keep you updated. We have more than one emergency beacon going off."

Betty immediately starts praying for the safety of her son and his crew. She makes tea and sits by the phone, waiting for more information. When the phone rings, she jumps, then picks up the receiver, hoping for good news. Instead, the Coast Guard coordinator asks her to tell him everything she knows about JP's proposed voyage. After they talk, Betty thinks of JP and how tough his life has been. She remembers the cruelty of her former husband toward his son and JP's close call with Hurricane Bertha. But she also thinks of his newfound happiness with Mayke and their home in the mountains. *Mayke! I should call Mayke.* She reaches for the phone. *Wait. Don't do it. There's nothing she can do, and this will just terrify her.*

Betty starts cleaning the house to keep busy, though her mind envisions huge black waves on a storm-tossed sea.

CHAPTER NINE

THE WAVE

On board the *Sean Seamour II,* the men are recovering from the shock of their capsizing. After activating the GPIRB, JP begins to assess the conditions inside the boat. He checks the portholes, then looks at the mast, where it comes down through the deck to rest on the keel support grid, and both are in good shape. There is some water in the bilge, but he is able to quickly pump it out. He assumes that water is entering through the air cowls whenever waves break on the transom. JP asks Ben and Rudy to sit on the floor on the starboard side of the vessel. The waves are beating against the port side, and he takes this precautionary measure so that no one is hurled from port to starboard if another rogue wave bears down on the boat.

Checking the instruments, JP sees that the winds are out of the northeast, and he shudders to think what might have happened to the vessel if they were directly inside the Gulf Stream. The wind and waves are moving the boat at a steady clip of six knots toward the south-southwest. Though the Gulf Stream is to their west, JP calculates that they are well removed from it and in no immediate danger of being pushed back into it. They are, however, in a massive Gulf Stream warm-water eddy, and there is nothing they can do about it.

There is nothing else to be done, so they sit quietly, waiting out the storm. No one can sleep with the wild motion of the boat and the ominous bangs on the hull from breaking waves. As the minutes go by, each man is lost in his own thoughts. JP assumes that the Coast Guard is working with an Amver vessel to come to the *Sean Seamour II*'s rescue.

As the night progresses toward three a.m., JP makes a rudder adjustment. He wants to keep the port side slightly more exposed to the waves than the stern for better stability in sync with the drogue, which was fed off the stern. The boat does not respond as he expects it to, and he is puzzled by the loss of control. Lurching to a porthole in the galley, he can see that the drogue line is taut, assumes it is still attached, but wonders about the lack of control. He also wonders why the Coast Guard has not called on the Iridium satellite phone. He moves to the chart table, takes a seat, and decides to call the Coast Guard, hoping there is a satellite in reception range.

Before he has time to make the call, the boat starts to roll. It passes the 45-degree mark, and the men hold their breath as their eyes widen in fear and disbelief. For a brief, agonizing second, time seems to stop. They feel that they are carried by some unearthly force as the boat continues to turn beyond the 90-degree mark and their world goes upside down. It's a surreal, sickening feeling, even worse than the first knockdown, because this is happening more slowly, giving them time to realize the pure horror of it all. The lights flicker, and there is a low rumble gaining volume coming from beyond the confines of the cabin. The rolling motion accelerates and seemingly defies gravity as objects are hurled from one side of the vessel to the other, crashing upon impact. Rudy and Ben are awkwardly pitched into a tumble as the *Sean Seamour II* does a complete 180-degree roll, caught inside the vortex of the wave. JP also starts to fall but is simultaneously slammed by the heavy salon table that has come free of its legs.

Buckets of green seawater flood into the upside-down sailboat.

The vessel has been struck by a colossal rogue wave that marine experts will later estimate is a minimum of eighty feet tall. It is possible that two waves joined forces to create one mass of energy—however it formed, there is no question about its power as it swallows the *Sean Seamour II,* whose mast is now pointing toward the bottom of the ocean.

JP struggles to breathe. Although his head is above the rising water, the impact from the falling table has broken seven ribs, and he's in excruciating pain. Then he feels the water climb up the back side of his neck and head, followed by silence as his ears submerge. He frantically fights to free himself, but he's pinned by the tabletop. *I'm going to drown inside my own boat!* Every neuron and nerve in his body is firing, sending adrenaline coursing through his limbs, but he cannot move.

Rudy is prone on the ceiling, which has become the floor of the capsized vessel. It takes him a couple of seconds to process what has happened. A single wall lamp is still on, and the first thing he sees is water shooting through two air vents as if someone is outside with a fire hose. Then he hears shouts: "Help! Help!" He looks toward the cries and, in the dim light, can see a mess of debris, including the tabletop. The top half of JP's head is barely visible above water.

Ben is also disoriented, but JP's hollering snaps him back to reality, and he heads toward the shouting. With Rudy, he pushes the table off JP and pulls the captain's head and shoulders out of the water. JP winces and groans as sharp pain spreads through his chest; slowly, he gets to his feet.

Almost two feet of water is sloshing about, with more gushing up through the ceiling vents below them. Aside from the incoming water, all is quiet. A couple of minutes go by as each man gathers himself and begins to process what has occurred. Ben is waiting for the vessel to right itself, but nothing happens. *There might be so much water inside, it's offsetting the weight of the keel.* One thought races through his mind: *I don't want to die trapped inside. Rather die topside. See the sky one last time.* Rudy is having the same thought, and he stumbles to where the sliding companionway hatch should be. He takes off his personal flotation device (PFD), which had hydrostatically inflated, but JP steps toward him and grabs him by the shoulders, and croaks, "Stay here!"

JP manages to ignore the throbbing in his chest. He's got one thing on his mind. The life raft. *Is it still with the boat? If the boat doesn't right itself, we're going to need it.* He looks down where the companionway should be and takes a big breath of air. Searing pain shoots through his ribs. Then he lowers himself into the three feet of water and disappears.

Ben and Rudy stare down at the spot where JP submerged himself. A minute goes by and he does not surface. Water sloshes from one side of the vessel to another, carrying all manner of debris. Rudy kneels down in the water, then sticks his head under and starts to pull his body toward where he believes the companionway hatch should be. He can't see a thing, and he gropes around, trying to feel for either JP or the hatch. He's running out of air and comes back to the surface. He shakes his head at Ben, indicating the futility of his dive. The two men look each other directly in the eye. It is their absolute lowest moment. *Did JP get stuck? Is he drowned? Did the waves take him away?* A creeping panic rises between them, spawned by the feeling that they are entombed. And the water is rising.

JP somehow manages to slide open the hatch and swim out, barely able to hold his breath. He needs air, yet he doesn't shoot directly for the surface; instead, he lets his hands feel their way to the starboard leg of the arch that rises from the stern of the boat, not far from the companionway hatch. He sweeps with his arm, feeling for the life raft canister, and follows the arch to the port side. Still no raft. It should be in the canister just a few inches aft of the arch. His lungs are screaming for air, and he's fighting their call. He can sense that his body will ignore the commands from his brain to hold his breath and that his mouth will open on its own.

Grabbing hold of the toe rail, JP plans to pull himself toward the surface by following the upside-down hull. Suddenly, the boat starts to right itself. It all happens so fast that there is no time to think, and JP holds on as best he can. Incredibly, he lands in a heap in the cockpit next to the helm as the boat rolls out of its capsized position.

Coughing, gagging, and desperately sucking in big gulps of air, the captain is exhausted and disoriented. Five or six seconds go by before he notices a dim light coming from an opening, and he realizes that he's in the cockpit, looking down the companionway steps. The light is coming from the cabin. Hope! The *Sean Seamour II* has something left in her; she's not done yet. A new shot of adrenaline courses through his body, temporarily blocking out the pain of the broken ribs.

Then he remembers that the raft is gone, and his spirits plunge as quickly as they rose. He glances under the arch at an empty space where the raft and canister were mounted on the boat. *Without the raft, we are as good as dead. The boat is on borrowed time.*

The battered captain steals another look down the companionway and realizes the top part of the companionway hatch is gone. He shouts down to Ben and Rudy, "Get the pumps running! I've got to find the raft!"

As JP's eyes adjust to the darkness, he takes a second to collect himself, kneeling in the pulpit area of the cockpit, which is just forward of the wheel. The *Sean Seamour II* is a bit more stable in the raging seas now that it is filled with thousands of pounds of water. A wave slides beneath, and when the boat is in the bottom of the canyon, it is eerily quiet, almost serene, giving JP the feeling that he and his crew are the last humans alive on the planet. Then the next wave carries the vessel up to the wind-whipped summit, where his senses are blasted by the roar of breaking seas. With a smudge of moonlight filtering through the cloud cover, he can see the outlines of the mountainous waves and white water at their crests. The sight is so incredible, so unlike anything he's ever seen, that he has to force himself to look away and focus on the boat. That's when he notices that the mast has been cracked, just above deck level, off its base. It is lying off to the port side of the boat, almost parallel to the hull, its lower half resting on top of the vessel and its upper half in the water. The rigging is a complete mess.

JP squints at the water beneath where the mast is lying. *The raft!* He can't believe it. The raft is fully inflated and pinned against the water by a spreader that extends from the main mast at a right angle. How the raft wasn't snatched away by the waves borders on the miraculous. Equally astounding, the raft is not the type that can be hydrostatically inflated by contact with water; it will inflate only when someone yanks on the trip line, or tether. The only plausible explanation for its inflation is that the canister came loose during the capsizing and started to drop toward the bottom of the ocean but stopped when it reached the end of the trip line. It likely remained in that position until the boat righted itself, causing enough tension on the line to trigger the carbon dioxide cartridges that inflated the raft, bursting it from the canister. Fortunately, the motion of the vessel wasn't enough to break the tether, and the raft stayed by the boat with the aid of the spreader mast lying on top of it. But now, to be able to use the raft, JP will have to remove it from beneath the spreader.

The captain is so determined that for now he is keeping fear at bay. He doesn't stop to think about the fact that he is not tethered to the

Sean Seamour II and could be thrown off at any second. He inches toward the raft. It appears to be upside down, and the ballast bags that normally hang beneath the raft and fill with water for stabilization are on the top, and one of them looks to be pierced by the spreader.

JP has a high tolerance for pain, having experienced the severe burns in childhood, but now the adrenaline rush is wearing off, and every movement of the boat causes agony that can't be ignored.

He knows the pain will soon become debilitating. In order to survive, JP must free the raft immediately.

CHAPTER TEN

THE LIFE RAFT

JP's resourcefulness seems to be a natural gift, just like his hero Robin Lee Graham, on the *Dove*. And like JP, Graham was asleep in his bunk on board the *Dove* when, at two-thirty a.m., he heard a rumbling noise and thought his boat had collided with a log or an uncharted reef. He raced topside and found to his horror that the mast was broken about six feet up, and most of it was in the water, dragging next to the heaving boat. While sleeping, he had worn his safety harness, but with the boom now overboard he had to remove the harness so he could get it and the sails back on board before they were lost for good. As he struggled with the mast, a large wave slammed the boat, sending Graham tumbling off the deck and into the sea with no lifeline. It was the first time in his life that he had fallen overboard.

Luckily, the boat wasn't drifting faster than he could swim, and he was able to get himself on board. Then, over a two-hour period, he was able to hack away at the rigging and retrieve the boom and sails while freeing the broken mast and letting it sink. When he went into the cabin, he was shivering from the cold. In his book *Dove,* he wrote: "Slowly I began to see that I was in real trouble. Now my muscles ached and I couldn't go to sleep as I thought of the mess I was in. My best chance was a jury rig and hope for good trade winds. Of course, if the winds failed I could drift in this ocean until they found my bones." The next day Graham cobbled together a small mast and sail, making a second small foresail of awning and patching it with a hand towel and shirt. For the next twenty-four days, he sailed his battered and broken boat until he made landfall and safety.

Perhaps JP's learning about Graham's ingenuity at such a young age rubbed off. From surviving the brutalities of his father, to learning to live in a country where he couldn't speak a word of the language, and somehow outlasting Hurricane Bertha when all seemed lost, JP had never been one to panic. Now he would have to do it again.

Crouched in the pelting rain and spray, JP is shivering. Because they are in an eddy of the Gulf Stream, the water is relatively warm— 69 degrees—but the wind, out of the northeast, is cold, especially against his wet skin. He squints at the raft on the port side of the sailboat pinned under the rigging from the fallen mast. Its canopy is torn; it undulates behind the raft with each passing wave. JP fears that if he doesn't get the raft free and secured to the boat quickly, it, too, will tear and deflate in a matter of seconds. He considers calling Ben and Rudy to help him lift the mast and rigging, then realizes that they will have difficulty finding their harnesses and tethers in the mess below. He would never forgive himself if one of the men were to be swept away from the boat after responding to his request. He sets about trying to free the raft himself.

When a wave rolls beneath the boat, JP notices that the mast rises up a bit higher because the buoyant life raft lifts the rig. He decides to use the waves to his advantage. Because part of the mast is on the poop deck, which is higher than the aft deck, there is a foot of space between the mast and the aft deck. The stanchions and lifeline encircling the boat are also supporting the mast, allowing space beneath it.

Crawling on his belly, JP inches his way into the opening. If the mast shifts or the stanchion supporting it gives way, he will be trapped.

Lying beneath the mast on his stomach and facing aft, JP is now at the port stern corner of the boat, with the raft only inches away. He reaches out and touches the raft with his right foot; he plans to lift the mast and shove it free of the rigging. With the aid of his left leg, he arches his back and boosts the mast, synchronizing his movement with a passing wave. Piercing pain radiates from his broken ribs, and he cries out as he kicks the raft. It doesn't budge. Another wave comes and he tries again, but the raft won't move. He cannot push it far enough to free it from the spreader entangled with the ballast bag.

Panting, he squeezes out from beneath the mast and stares at the raft, knowing he has to somehow cut the bag from the spreader mast. He has shut out the roar of the crashing waves and ignores the drenching he gets when a wave breaks on the vessel. His mind races. *I don't have a knife, and there is no time to get one. The raft is going to rip apart at any minute, and when it loses its air, we are done for.*

He grabs the ballast bag, yanking with all his strength. He can't hear the tear, but he can feel it. He moves his hands farther up the bag and, taking a deep and painful breath, pulls back hard. Again he feels the bag give way. He can see the spreader in its entirety and knows he has freed the bag. Only the weight of the spreader and wire stays is on the raft. JP slides back into the opening between the mast and the deck. He resumes his position and, with his left leg, pushes the mast upward while shoving the raft with his right leg. At last the raft bobs free of the rigging.

Just as JP begins to lower the mast, an especially large wave breaks directly on him, and the mast is pushed down on the left side of his back, crushing him against the deck. He moans in agony. Another three ribs are broken.

Somehow he is able to inch out from beneath the mast where he collapses on the deck, water swirling around his body. Lying there, he worries about going into shock, which would waste all of his efforts. The raft is bouncing wildly with each wave, slamming into the hull and then being carried away from the boat—JP knows he must get it starboard for safe boarding.

Fighting through the pain, he forces himself into a crouching position and grabs the tether attached to the raft. He plans to crawl toward the bow, pulling the raft along, then securing it to the opposite side of the boat. A flashback to his sailing accident in Hurricane Bertha gives him pause. He remembers how exposed the bow can be when waves are crashing upon it and how difficult that made it to stay on board. And now with no safety harness, he realizes that if he leaves the cockpit, he'll likely be swept overboard.

He can't walk the raft around the stern because the protruding mast extends beyond the back of the boat. He decides to lift the raft from one side of the vessel to the other. He tries to pull the raft up over the stanchion, but it is so heavy that it barely moves. Shifting position onto his back, he gets one leg under the raft and, pulling with his hands, he is able to get part of it out of the water and on the stanchion. Using the waves for leverage, he edges more of the raft out of the water.

A gust of wind catches the raft. The raft comes completely out of the water and flips right over the cockpit, landing upside down on the starboard side. JP, clutching the tether, can't believe his good fortune. He secures the raft to the side of the boat.

Sitting in the cockpit, JP thinks through what should be done next. He wants to wait until the last possible moment to put his crew on the raft. The violence of the waves and the raft's missing canopy mean it will not be an easy ride. *We've got to stay with the boat. We can't leave until I know for sure she is sinking.*

He peers out at the deck, awash in foam and green water, resolving to do whatever he can to keep the *Sean Seamour II* afloat just a little bit longer. He crawls back toward the mast and examines it more closely. It cracked about four inches above the deck and is almost completely severed. JP thinks it will be easy to hack through the rest of the crack. Most of the stays and shrouds have been shorn away, and the two that remain can be freed with the bolt cutters. He wants to dump the mast and rigging into the ocean so the boat will ride more evenly and gain some buoyancy. He's also worried that the mast or spreader will puncture the hull if it shifts.

Glancing at the bow, he guesses that the anchor chain is hanging over the side, pulling the vessel down with its half ton of weight. The bolt cutters should be able to sever the chain. He thinks that if he can find a safety harness and tether, he might try to free the boat of the drifting anchor and chain.

Moving to the companionway, JP can see Rudy and Ben bailing water below in the dim light. He starts down the stairs, ready to tell his crew about the raft and his plan to cut the mast and anchor free. His eyes go to the GPIRB, still in its cradle. He freezes. There is no light coming from the GPIRB. It is dead.

CHAPTER ELEVEN

DESPERATION

The *Sean Seamour II* isn't the first vessel to have GPIRB/EPIRB issues. As far back as 1980, there was a survival ordeal during a storm in the Gulf Stream that was eerily similar. The vessel was the *Polar Bear,* captained by Peter Reich on a voyage from Shelter Island, New York, bound for the Caribbean in late October. Reich and his sailing partner, Andy Reeve, were on board the *Polar Bear,* a Luders thirty-three-foot sailboat—the same model that Robin Lee Graham sailed on the second half of his trip. Like Graham, Reich and Reeve, ages twenty-three and twenty-four respectively, were young, but both had been sailing all their lives and had been in some nasty weather. Consequently, when the weather deteriorated during this voyage, the two men were not concerned and instead enjoyed the bracing ride. But as the weather went from bad to worse, and they had reduced their sails until they were drifting with bare poles, they realized that a storm in the Gulf Stream was unlike anything they had experienced. They were more than four hundred miles off Montauk, Long Island, and five hundred miles off Cape May, New Jersey.

They had lashed the tiller in place and sealed themselves in the belly of the boat when disaster struck. "I thought a ship hit us," recalls Peter, "the bang was so loud. The boat rolled to almost a complete knockdown, and we were tossed like rag dolls. Gear inside the boat flew like missiles." Both men had been thrown violently across the cabin, with Andy landing on the dinette, breaking it in half. All power was lost. The two men decided, in order to avoid another knockdown, that they should raise a small storm sail and stream a sea anchor. They would have to go out on deck and then remain in the cockpit, where they could man the tiller. They tethered themselves to the vessel, but another monster wave broke directly on the boat, knocking it on its side. The two sailors found themselves swept off the boat and into the ocean. Peter was towed through the water, and when the boat righted, he found himself hanging upside down from the boom by his harness. Andy, who had crawled back into the boat, unhooked his friend, who then dropped onto the cockpit.

They scrambled down into the cabin, where water was slowly rising, coming in from cracks in the companionway hatch. The bilge pumps were clogging with debris, so the sailors manually bailed. To throw the water out of the boat, they needed to open the companionway hatch, and that meant almost as much water was coming back in. Peter decided the boat was slowly sinking, and he activated the EPIRB.

It was now about three p.m., and they needed to decide if being in the cabin was any safer than being on deck. When they thought of the items flying through the air in the cabin and the possibility of being trapped inside, they took their chances on deck, where they could begin to prepare the life raft. Waves were sweeping over the deck, and the rails were awash. By looking up at the forty-foot mast, they estimated the waves were fifty to sixty feet.

The life raft was a four-person Avon model with a canopy above and small ballast bags below. As they inflated the raft, Peter feared it would be blown away like a kite, and he scrambled to get a strong line attached to it. "The painter to the life raft was only a quarter inch wide," says Peter, "and I thought for sure it would break. I tied another line to it and secured it as best I could next to the boat. Andy then started handing me food, water, and gear from below, and I stowed it in the raft. Then the strangest thing happened."

From out of the gloom of driving rain and flying foam, Peter saw a ship coming toward them. He could not believe that just twenty minutes after activating the EPIRB, it had resulted in a ship coming to their rescue. *This EPIRB is amazing,* he thought. He grabbed some flares, but the first three or four—all brand-new—didn't fire. But the next couple did. The ship kept coming. Peter noticed that it wasn't slowing down; nor was it veering toward them. He realized the men on the ship didn't even see his boat, and had not been sent by the Coast Guard, because there was no way the EPIRB signal could have resulted in a ship diverting to them so soon. He watched the ship plow by. On or near its pilothouse, he could see what looked like four letters indicating the name of the ship, but with all the rain, he couldn't make it out clearly. Then it was gone.

In all probability, the ship that went by was the *Poet,* a 523-foot freighter steaming from Philadelphia to Egypt. Andy and Peter could not believe the ship never saw their flares, but in hindsight, it proved to be a blessing for the two men. The storm sank the *Poet.* It literally disappeared without a trace, taking its thirty-four sailors to the bottom of the sea. Officials never determined what happened to the ship or where it met its demise, but Peter believes the monster waves in the Gulf Stream were the culprit. Maybe its cargo load shifted, maybe its hull was breached, or maybe it lost engine power and took one too many waves beam-on.

Watching the ship go by and eventually out of view was a sickening feeling for Peter and Andy, but the two men didn't have time to dwell on it. Their boat was listing badly, and waves were covering the deck. It was going to sink at any moment. The two sailors entered the raft and cut it free from the boat, and the waves separated them from the vessel.

Night came on. Neither man had slept in forty-eight hours, so they huddled together and fell into a fitful sleep. Sometime during the night, the raft flipped completely over, and the men woke up to find themselves underwater. Totally disoriented, they struggled in the darkness, freed themselves from the raft, and kicked to the surface. Luckily, they emerged from the water next to the raft and hung on to one of its outside lines, exhausted and coughing up seawater. They worked together to get the raft right side up, knowing they would die from hypothermia if they couldn't get out of the water. After several attempts, they succeeded in turning the raft and crawled inside. In the darkness, they felt around the inside of the raft with their hands, frantically searching for their food and supplies, and were horrified to find it swept virtually clean by the capsizing. All that was left was a liter of ginger ale, eight slices of cheese, three oranges, and a canned ham.

That night was the longest of Peter's life. But when dawn came, the seas started to abate. They had survived the storm, but could they survive hypothermia, dehydration, and starvation? The two castaways allowed themselves each a sip of ginger ale in the morning and one at night. Peter wondered why he had not heard any Coast Guard planes, and he examined the EPIRB. Another shock—water had gotten inside the unit, corroding its electronics and battery. From the looks of the corrosion, he suspected that it had been compromised much earlier than this ill-fated trip. Peter and Andy looked at each other, knowing that help would not be coming and that it would take an incredible stroke of luck to survive.

For the next five days and nights, the two men did their best to hang on. Nights were particularly difficult as they huddled in a sodden sleeping bag and shivered. Peter stuffed a corner of the sleeping bag into his mouth to keep his teeth from chattering.

On the fifth night, they saw the range lights of a ship in the distance and realized it was a good seven miles off and not coming any closer. They scrambled to get the flares out, then tried to shoot them off. Flare after flare would not fire. One last flare was a parachute flare, which, when ignited, should fire from its tube like a bazooka. When Peter activated the flare, it only fizzled. He could not believe that salvation was so close and this last flare wouldn't ignite. As he started to lower the tube, the flare went off, but because the tube was pointed at a 45-degree angle rather than straight up, the flare's parachute ride back to the ocean was a short one. Would the ship see it?

A sailor on the ship spotted the flare just before it was extinguished in the ocean. The captain immediately sounded the ship's horn, and then all the lights came on. The ship headed toward where they saw the flare and found the two marooned sailors in the raft. When they were aboard the ship, they tried to take a step but collapsed.

The ship's captain radioed the Coast Guard that they had found two men adrift in a life raft. It was then that Peter's fear about the damaged EPIRB was confirmed: The Coast Guard had never gotten a distress signal. At the time it was Coast Guard policy not to mount a search for any vessel overdue if it had an EPIRB on board that was never activated.

Inspection of the EPIRB told them that water had indeed seeped into the unit, which resulted in the corrosion and loss of power. As a result of this harrowing incident, the manufacturer issued a recall notice explaining that "EPIRB units may not be watertight." EPIRBs are an absolute must on boats that go far offshore, but like any man-made device, they are not infallible, and a tiny fraction fail.

Between the faulty EPIRB, the flares that were duds, and the waves that were so big they flipped the life raft despite its ballast bags, Peter and Andy were indeed lucky. Yet their biggest stroke of luck might have been when the doomed cargo ship *Poet* steamed right by without ever seeing the life raft.

Luck. JP, Rudy, and Ben are going to need it. The GPIRB is dead, the boat is slowly sinking, and the raft is damaged.

JP has the yellow GPIRB in his hand, shaking it, turning the switch on and off again and again to reinitialize it, but still there is no light to indicate it is transmitting. *Did it ever send a signal?* he wonders. *When did it go dead?* Part of him doesn't want to tell the crew, but when he carries it down into the cabin, they know something is wrong by the look on his face. Then they see that the GPIRB's strobe is not working.

"It's dead," says JP. "Maybe since the second capsizing. I've got to see about the radios. The life raft is secured to the boat, but its canopy is gone, and so are its ballast bags. We've got to stay with the boat as long as we can."

Rudy and Ben don't say a word. So much has happened in such a short period of time that they feel partly numb to the latest news. While JP was topside, they had been steadily bailing, throwing the water out the open companionway. Ben ingeniously cut the bottom out of a large water container to use as a scoop, and Rudy soon did the same. They didn't stop bailing when JP reentered the cabin, but despite their efforts, they can only stay even with the water entering the boat through the broken companionway hatch, the mast hole, and the breached portholes. At least the water coming in through the air vents has largely stopped now that the boat has enough water inside that the pressure is equalized.

Rudy pauses for a moment. His back, hurt from being thrown out of bed, seizes up, and he needs to rest. Two pumps are running, but both are continually clogging with debris and shutting down. Rudy realizes that they can't keep bailing indefinitely; soon the incoming water will overwhelm them. He wonders if they will have any warning when the boat begins its descent to the bottom of the sea. As if answering his thought, a large wave slams the boat, knocking the men off their feet and into a bulkhead.

Rudy regains his footing and goes back to bailing, pausing only to snatch a floating apple, which he eats, thinking it may be some time before he sees food again.

JP is looking over the rest of his communications equipment. The Iridium phone is soaked and out of commission, as is the single-side band radio. The primary VHF radio is also useless because its antenna, located on top of the mast, is lying in the water. Stored away on the boat is a backup antenna that inserts into a dedicated plug, but it is impossible to find in the sloshing mess of the cabin.

The boat does have two handheld VHF units that are still working. JP picks one up. "Mayday, Mayday, Mayday," he says. "This is the sailing vessel *Sean Seamour II*." He listens, not really expecting any answer. In good weather, JP estimates the handheld VHF might broadcast thirty miles, but in the storm, he figures ten miles is its maximum range.

JP explains to Ben and Rudy that the handheld VHF radio is working, but its range is next to nothing. Still, periodically, one of the men will pick it up and call out Maydays, hoping for a miracle.

It is now about four a.m., and the sailors are utterly exhausted. Rudy, not understanding the full extent of the damage to the raft, approaches JP and says, "Maybe we should think about getting into the raft." The captain shakes his head. "Let's wait longer, until we are sure the boat is sinking."

JP tries to help Rudy and Ben bail, but with broken ribs, he is unable to lift the scoop high enough to throw water out the companionway. He feels himself slowing down, wondering if he is going into shock. He is in pain, but even worse is the feeling that his thought process is beginning to cloud over. *Could this be hypothermia?* Whatever is happening scares him and stirs up waves of despair. His thoughts are not on just his own survival but also that of his crew, and he wonders what more he can do. He has long since given up the idea to cut the mast and anchor chain free because he was unable to find a harness and tether, and even if he did, his strength is so low that he doesn't feel he could do the job. His options are shrinking.

Too feeble and faint to bail, JP posts himself near one of the pumps to keep its intake free of debris. He tries to think through the evacuation into the life raft. He monitors his boat's buoyancy by occasionally poking his head outside the top of the companionway, letting his eyes adjust to mixed moonlight and cloud, and peering toward the bow. *When the anchor roller is underwater, it's time to go. But not a moment before.* He tells himself to stick to this plan no matter how strong the urge gets to leave the boat.

JP is hoping to avoid a life raft boarding in the dark, knowing that would pose double the danger. For the next hour, he monitors the waterline and notes that the water is slowly creeping upward. *Just hang on until daylight,* he says both to himself and to the *Sean Seamour II*.

Suddenly, at about five-thirty, two large waves crash directly on the boat, sending it careening down the face of the wave. The men are thrown to the starboard side, but amazingly, no one is injured. The boat, however, doesn't fare as well. Green water blasts down the companionway, filling the vessel with an additional foot of seawater, bringing the level above the men's knees.

JP climbs the companionway, and from the cockpit he can see that the bow of his beloved boat is submerged. Holding his broken ribs, he turns and shouts back down toward Rudy and Ben. "Let's go! It's time to get out!"

CHAPTER TWELVE

INTO THE SEA

Boarding a life raft is fraught with danger. The first concern is the timing. You want to be in the life raft before the boat goes down, but not a minute before—a damaged boat is still safer than a life raft. The motion inside a boat is not as violent, and the boat is almost always dryer, which is crucial to warding off hypothermia. Keeping your body out of the water or at least partially dry is paramount, because water sucks away body heat twenty-five times faster than air.

When it comes to being rescued, the boat is also a better bet than a life raft because it is a bigger target for searchers in a plane or a passing ship. And the boat might have at least one radio working, allowing those in Mayday situations to broadcast as long as possible or maybe communicate with rescuers about the details and preparation for rescue.

Life rafts may have some survival gear, but the boat will have far more. The boat will likely have extra food, water, a first-aid kit, clothes, PFDs, and flares, and of course, the life raft and its supplies will be with the boat as well. Once you are in the life raft, both supplies and options shrink, and if the life raft gets flipped, the supplies might be swept away.

The old maritime saying "You've got to step up to the life raft" is a good one, reminding sailors not to board until they know the boat is sinking. But pithy sayings are difficult to follow in the actual chaos of a storm. On the flip side, if you wait too long to exit the vessel, there may not be enough time. Boats can and do sink suddenly. One minute a vessel can be slowly losing its battle to the sea, with water inching inside, and the next the bow plunges downward, the stern rears up, and the entire boat starts its slide to the bottom of the ocean.

All one can do is process the information as best as he or she can, then decide when the danger of staying on the boat exceeds that of being in a life raft. Factor in incredible fatigue or seasickness, and the right decision gets even more difficult.

Entering the life raft has its own set of risks. Most mariners practice evacuation drills, but under calm conditions. A storm is anything but calm, and hurricane-force winds and crashing seas pose a unique set of challenges. Assuming you are able to stay on a deck that is pitching like a bronco and free the raft canister from its mounting, you must then shove it into the water and yank the painter that pulls the pin from the carbon dioxide device that inflates the raft. This is where the trouble usually begins. The inflated raft takes off like a kite in the wind, and holding on to a thin painter becomes a real challenge. The line can cut into the hands, and getting the raft back to the boat can be extremely difficult, if not impossible. All the while you worry that the painter, which is designed to part from the raft if enough pressure is applied, will hold. (It is constructed that way so that if the boat starts sinking and one end of the painter is secured to the raft and the other to the boat, the painter will give way before the raft gets pulled down with the boat.)

If you do get the raft next to the boat, the objective—to lessen the chance or the pace of hypothermia—will be to board it without getting wet. This is almost impossible in a storm. The raft, even one with a canopy, may already be filled with water from waves crashing into its doorway. Even if the raft is dry, chances are you will end up in the water while trying to board. On a heaving deck, you would have to crawl toward the raft and either make a perfect headfirst dive into the raft's doorway, or sit on the edge of the boat and crawl inside if you can time the waves just right. More likely, you will need to swim to the raft and pull yourself in, soaking and shivering.

JP, Rudy, and Ben know they are going to get wet because the raft's canopy is gone, and the waves, at least seventy feet in size, will punish the raft like a little cork going down a raging river.

As the men prepare to climb out of the cabin, Rudy puts his wallet and passport in a plastic zip bag. "What the heck are you doing?" says Ben. "We're probably going to die, and we won't be needing those."

Ben has already come to terms with the notion that they won't be getting out of this jam. With the GPIRB not working, and the old EPIRB not equipped with a hydrostatic release, he figures the Coast Guard never received their distress signal. And even if they did, Ben knows the only hope of rescue is by helicopter, and he knows the winds are too strong for one to enter the storm. The only alternative is to give up, but he wants to go down fighting, wants to see the sky one last time. Rudy and JP, too, feel that their ultimate fate is death, but they're going to try to stay alive as long as they can.

All three men are calm as they prepare to exit the boat and enter into the void. They tie themselves together with the tethers from their safety harnesses, hoping to avoid separation should they fall out of the raft. Rudy puts on the PFD he took off earlier, then stuffs his pockets with flares and a steak knife for cutting the raft free from the boat.

JP sees that his mates are ready. "Let's go," he says, slowly starting up the companionway steps, lugging a ditch bag with survival supplies behind him. In the bag is a handheld VHF radio, the Iridium satellite phone with extra batteries, food, water, flares, and other items necessary for survival at sea and assisting with rescue. Ben is next to climb the stairs. When it is Rudy's turn, he takes a last look around and grabs the dead GPIRB. He thinks, *We have nothing else, and even though it's dead, I might as well take it.*

When JP crawls into the cockpit, the tempest assaults him with shrieking wind and crashing seas. Thankfully, a gray dawn light helps them see, and JP notes with relief that the upside-down life raft is still secured to the vessel.

Ben and Rudy climb into the cockpit and get their first good look at the avalanching waves. Ben cannot believe the size of the white-capped mountains of water surrounding him. One minute a wave towers above the boat; the next minute the vessel rises to the top, where Ben surveys foam-streaked waves in all directions. He has never seen such raw power, the absolute height of nature's fury, and he is awestruck.

The main line from the life raft to the boat is in a winch, and JP, standing on the elevated poop deck with his back against the steel arch, frees it. By pulling on the line toward the port stern side of the boat, he manages to flip the raft right side up. He gasps for air, which causes him to wince in pain from the slight pressure on his ribs. Suddenly his eyes widen as he sees that the line that was fastened to the drogue has severed a foot beyond where it was tied to a cleat on the boat. It is a clean break, and JP surmises it must have snapped like a rubber band during the first knockdown. There is no time to wonder if the vessel might have avoided the second disastrous capsizing had the drogue not snapped free—the bow of the boat is now completely submerged.

The raft is tight against the hull. With no canopy, and the boat riding low in the water, JP slides beneath the lifeline circling the boat and drops down into the raft. Ben follows and then Rudy.

Rudy realizes how exposed to the elements they will be. They sit in a flat area surrounded by an inflated tube; he likens it to being in a bathtub. He doesn't want to think about what will happen when they release from the boat.

Six inches of water splash about inside the raft. The water temperature is 70 degrees Fahrenheit and does not feel cold to Rudy or Ben. They know they are lucky to be at the eastern edge of the Gulf Stream; if they were just a few miles off the western side instead, the May temperature of the ocean would be 60 degrees or lower.

The tether securing the raft to the boat needs to be cut, and Rudy does the job with the steak knife. Then he holds up the knife and looks at JP, who shouts, "Toss it! We don't want any sharp objects on the raft." Rudy quickly drops it into the ocean. The raft, however, does not float free of the sailboat. Waves batter it against the vessel, sending the men colliding against one another. Rudy, now on his knees, leans toward the sailboat and pushes the raft away as hard as he can. The raft bounces right back into the boat, sending Rudy backward into Ben. Twice more Rudy pushes against the boat, but the raft moves only three feet before slamming into the hull. The men frantically scan the outside of the raft. Rudy sees that there is a line leading back to the shredded canopy, which is caught on the *Sean Seamour II*. *Oh no,* thinks Rudy, *we have nothing to cut it with!*

Ben grabs Rudy's shoulder. Rudy turns to look at him and sighs with relief. Ben is holding up the rescue knife he purchased back in Jacksonville just a few days earlier. Since Rudy is sitting closest to the boat, he takes the knife from Ben and cuts the last remaining line. Rudy observes that the sailboat is nose-down in the water.

A wave rolls under the raft, pushing it away, blocking the men's view of the sailboat. As the wave passes, the men stare at where the boat should be. It is gone. The ocean has swallowed the *Sean Seamour II* into its dark and unforgiving depths.

CHAPTER THIRTEEN

THE CUTTER *TAMPA* AND THE C-130

The cutter *Tampa* is headed into the teeth of the storm, heading toward the coordinates from EPIRB hits transmitted by the *Flying Colours* and the *Sean Seamour II*. Waves batter the cutter, and the ninety-seven crewmen and women aboard are bracing themselves, struggling to maintain their positions. At least a third of the crew is seasick, and all are tired from trying to maintain their balance to offset the constant motion of the ship.

The 270-foot-long cutter left the coast of New Jersey a few hours earlier but is at least twenty-four hours away from the distress scene. The maximum speed of the cutter is twenty knots, but because they are steaming into waves of twenty feet, the fastest headway they can make is between fourteen and sixteen knots. Executive Officer Charles Fosse has never been in waves this large and menacing, and he can only imagine what they must be like closer to the Gulf Stream. Already some Coasties have cuts and bruises from being knocked off their feet when the seas rolled the vessel 30 degrees. During one particularly vicious hit from a wave, so much water avalanched on the deck that it entered the ventilation system and crew members felt like it was raining inside the cutter.

Sending a cutter on a rescue mission into a storm of this magnitude has its own set of risks. Take the case of the cutters *Bedloe* and *Jackson,* both 125 feet and weighing 220 tons. During a massive hurricane in September 1944, later named the Great Atlantic Hurricane, the two cutters were dispatched to aid a Liberty ship in distress just off the coast of North Carolina. Waves were topping out at eighty feet, and neither of the cutters could withstand the liquid walls of water tossing them about like so much flotsam. A few miles off

82

Oregon Inlet, both cutters suffered knockdowns and filled with so much water that they started to sink.

William Ruhl, aboard the *Jackson,* was in the galley when the ship began a roll and kept going over. Green seawater poured through a broken hatch, and Ruhl scrambled up the passageway onto the deck, forgetting his life jacket in the dash to escape being trapped. "The waves were like mountains rolling over the ship," he later recalled. The ship was on its side, and Ruhl was swimming in the ocean. Luckily, a raft, torn from the deck of the ship, was bobbing in the water nearby, and Ruhl heaved himself inside. Six other Coasties found their way into the tiny raft, but others were not so lucky.

In the raft, the survivors assumed that help would be coming from the *Bedloe* soon, not knowing that their sister ship had sunk as well. The men made it through the night, but when it became apparent that help was not imminent, two of them tried to swim ashore. They swam for three hours with little progress and turned back when they saw a shark circling.

For the next fifty hours, those six men bailed, prayed, and hung on as best they could. Coast Guard Kingfisher planes from Elizabeth City eventually spotted the raft and landed the aircraft in the swells. The aircrew shed their clothes, jumped into the water, and hoisted the survivors onto the wings of the plane, where they administered first aid while awaiting rescue boats from Oregon Inlet.

Two other rafts were located, and survivors explained that several men had died during the second night from exposure and exhaustion. William McCreedy was on board a rescue boat and recalled that when he approached one of the rafts, a man inside jumped overboard and became tangled in a trailing line. McCreedy dove into the water, cut the man free, and with the aid of crewmates, hoisted him into the boat. As they were heading back to shore with other survivors, the man who had jumped overboard touched McCreedy's face and said, "We made it." Those were his last words—a moment later, he died. A total of forty-eight Coasties from the *Jackson* and *Bedloe* perished during that ill-fated mission.

Now, in the storm that has sunk the *Sean Seamour II* and is trying to sink the *Illusion,* the *Flying Colours,* and the *Seeker,* the Coasties aboard the *Tampa* are putting themselves in grave peril.

• • •

Besides the *Tampa,* the other resource being sent into the storm is the Lockheed C-130 Hercules, a long-range fixed-wing aircraft, a real workhorse for the Coast Guard. This four-engine turboprop plane was originally designed as a troop, medical evacuation, and cargo transport plane. It has been in continuous production for more than fifty years, used primarily by the U.S. Air Force, the Marine Corps, and the Coast Guard. The Coast Guard has modified the aircraft for search and rescue as well as reconnaissance and patrol. Compared to the Coast Guard helicopters that work with the C-130 on rescue missions, the plane looks enormous, with a length of 97 feet, a wingspan of 132 feet, and an empty weight of 76,000 pounds.

The Coast Guard uses a crew of seven for C-130 rescue missions. In the flight deck, the pilot sits in the left seat, the copilot in the right, and directly behind them the flight mechanic. Next are two seats for the navigator and the radioman. Three steps down from the flight deck is the cavernous cargo compartment that holds the SAR bin, filled with life rafts, radios, survival suits, flares, and dewatering pumps. Two more Coasties sit in this area—the drop master and a basic air crewman. They can open the ramp door in the rear of the aircraft and push out pieces of survival equipment to people in distress below. Usually, this equipment is deployed by parachute unless the wind is extreme. If they need to drop flares or a data buoy marker that measures drift rates, they can open paratroop doors on either the left or right of the cargo compartment. When the drop master and basic air crewmen are not deploying equipment, they have access to two side windows from which they can assist the other crewmen scanning the ocean for survivors.

The C-130 flying toward the *Sean Seamour II* and *Flying Colours* is under the command of Paul Beavis, flight commander. He has a crew of six: Copilot Ed Ahlstrand, Flight Engineer Stacy Sorenson, Navigator Marcus Jones, Radioman Jesse Bennett, Drop Master Casey Green, and Air Crewman Ryan Cantu. When they launched from Norfolk, they climbed to an altitude of eighteen thousand feet, and Beavis instructed Marcus Jones to set a sector search based on the last EPIRB hits. They later will augment this search pattern with additional information sent from SAR Headquarters to account for drift rates and currents.

The farther out to sea they fly, the more turbulent the ride. Heavy rain begins to fall when they are one hundred miles out, and the crew knows the search won't be easy. When they are about fifty miles from the closest EPIRB hit, they begin descending, not stopping until they are below cloud cover at just four hundred feet above the ocean. The radioman begins making broadcasts, trying to hail one of the vessels in distress, but no one answers.

Dawn has provided a bit of light, but the rain makes visibility poor. The turbulence is severe, causing the plane to lurch. Jones braces himself to help stabilize his vision. He has been in the Coast Guard seven years and logged more than three thousand hours aboard C-130s, and he's never been in weather like this.

Through the rain-swept windshield, Commander Beavis gets his first look at the waves, and they are beyond anything he has encountered. He watches a wave break into a chaotic brew of crashing foam, and it appears that the white water stretches longer than a city block. They are now on-scene, and the aircraft is flying in racetrack-pattern loops, each extending farther from the center. It's the turns that put Beavis on edge. They have to roll the plane to a 30-degree angle on each turn. With wind blasts of eighty knots and their low proximity to the water, the commander has plenty to worry about. He's using every bit of concentration to keep the four-hundred-foot altitude steady and not bank too steeply. There's a fine line between keeping the plane low enough to have any hope at spotting a boat or raft, yet protecting it from the enormous waves, which could clip the wing closest to the water while they're banking. Beavis knows that the lives of his crew are in his hands, as well as the life of anyone on a boat below. He also knows that if any of the sailors are in the water, it will be nearly impossible to spot them. He's not even sure his crew can pick a life raft out of the cauldron below.

CHAPTER FOURTEEN

TUMBLING IN CHAOS

JP's beloved boat is gone, and with it, his outside link to the world. He stares at the empty spot in the ocean where the boat was just a couple of seconds earlier. He tries to think ahead and searches for the bright yellow grab bag he had filled with supplies. It, too, is gone. He remembers dropping it in the cockpit and shouting for one of the others to carry it into the raft while he released the tether from the winch. But with the shrieking wind and blinding spray, neither Rudy nor Ben heard JP or saw the bag. *It sank with the boat,* he thinks. It was much too heavy to float. Of all the supplies in the bag, the men most need water and flares; they have no other source of water, and JP is not sure if Rudy stuffed a few flares in his foul-weather gear at the last moment. Whatever survival supplies might have come pre-packaged with the raft have been swept away, probably when it was impaled by the mast and dragged next to the boat.

JP's brain and body seem to be crashing at the same time. He watches Rudy and Ben try to cover themselves with a small piece of canopy, though it is repeatedly blown away. In a weak voice, JP rasps, "It's useless." The lack of a canopy not only means the raft will stay full of water no matter how much they bail; it also reduces their odds of being spotted by a plane. The canopy is a bright fluorescent orange, but the raft itself is black and blends in with the dark ocean. Making matters worse is that without the ballast bags hanging below, the little vessel is less stable and more susceptible to flipping. It slides wildly with the waves, and whenever it reaches a crest, the men feel like they are at the apex of a roller-coaster ride during that split second of hang time before they plunge back down. They are afraid they will be thrown from the raft, so they use the clips at the end of their safety harness tethers to fasten themselves to a lifeline inside the raft.

Ben stares at the oncoming walls of water and is struck by the utter despair he feels in his surroundings: gray skies, gray waves, and white streaks of foam where the top of the giant combers meet the sky. The water is seething in every direction, and the only thing between the men and the lethal seas are the three fabric tubes encircling the floor of the raft.

None of the three men is talking. All have arrived at the same conclusion: *No one is coming for us.* Rudy thinks, *Even if we manage to stay in the raft, we aren't going to live long.* He glances at JP and notices the captain's skin color is a sickly gray, as if his blood isn't circulating properly. Rudy wonders if JP is in shock from his injury and if he has entered the early stages of hypothermia. He worries that his friend isn't going to make it another hour.

While the 70-degree water temperature might seem relatively warm, in time it will kill anyone who stays submerged or partially submerged. The first victim would be JP, because he is short and slim. When cold starts to suck away the body's heat, larger, heavier people fare much better than small, thin people. JP is also completely exhausted, which won't help in his battle to generate body heat. The first body parts to be affected are the fingers and toes, where there is little fat to insulate the blood from the heat-sapping water. These extremities will become numb and stiff, and JP will lose dexterity. In essence, the body yields these extremities to the cold, reducing blood flow to the area in an effort to keep the core—particularly the heart—warm. Next to go will be the arms and legs, making it hard to swim. If JP is swept from the raft at an advanced stage of hypothermia, he won't be able to stroke back, and he will die from drowning long before the loss of body heat causes his heart to give out. Many hypothermic victims lose consciousness and die when they can no longer keep their heads out of the water. This usually happens when the body's core temperature drops to 87 degrees.

Most people think that they must keep moving to keep the blood circulating and generate body heat, but that just expends precious energy. A person in cold water should conserve energy by minimizing movement. Loss of body heat can be slowed by holding your knees to your chest to help keep the upper torso warm. And two people can help fight off hypothermia by huddling together, chest to chest.

JP is helped by the fact that he is fully clothed in foul-weather gear, which traps a bit of body heat. But most of the body's warmth escapes from the head, and he has no hat on. If the raft's canopy were up, that would reduce the loss of heat from windchill, but JP is sitting and shivering in a half foot of water, completely exposed to the hurricane-force winds. The involuntary shivering is his body's way of trying to produce a little warmth in its fight against the cold.

Adding to the effects of hypothermia will be dehydration; it, too, causes the blood to thicken with decreased volume. The symptoms of dehydration include a reduction in mental abilities, slurred speech, and overall inefficiency—the same problems caused by hypothermia. A person needs two quarts of water a day to maintain health, and soon all three men will be parched. They will have to fight the urge to sip seawater, which only makes the problems worse—the salt dehydrates the body, causing hallucinations.

JP's slow-circulating blood is restricting the flow of oxygen to his brain, and that, along with shock, is the cause of his mental sluggishness. If the hypothermia advances, the blood will thicken further, making clear thought all but impossible. Help will have to come soon, or the hypothermia will continue its silent march toward his brain and vital organs.

For now, JP drifts in and out of consciousness. He has resigned himself to death—a feeling he remembers from the terrible burns of his childhood. He feels the same sad helplessness that he did at the burn hospital, knowing there is nothing more he can do for himself or his crew. The storm was just too much for him and his *Sean Seamour II*. He fights the urge to drift off for good. It's not time yet.

The raft, pushed by the wind and waves, is traveling at an incredible nine knots—it is already miles from the site where the EPIRB indicated the emergency. The sounds of the ocean rise and fall with the waves. When the sailors are in the trough, the crashing seas are muffled slightly, but as the raft rides toward the crest, the roaring increases until they teeter on the top and are exposed to the full fury of the howling wind.

TUMBLING IN CHAOS

After about twenty minutes in the raft, disaster strikes. An enormous wave slides under the raft, lifting it higher and higher. As the vessel nears the crest, the steep wave can no longer support itself and comes crashing down directly on the raft. It slams into the men with the impact of a train. The raft is flipped like a pancake, and the men go flying and tumbling. In the trough, Rudy and Ben, still tethered to the raft, realize they are under the overturned vessel, and they quickly unclip and kick to the surface. Salt stings their eyes as they search for JP. Rudy ducks beneath the raft to find him struggling with his tether. Rudy, not yet feeling any real effects of hypothermia, is able to unclip JP and bring him out from under the raft. Another wave towers over the men, ready to pounce and pile-drive them under and maybe finish them off. Thankfully, this second wave is not as steep as the first, and it doesn't break but instead slides under the three sailors. In the second trough, Rudy hears JP mumbling, and he leans closer. "Ben, Ben, where's Ben?" says JP.

"He's on the other side of the raft!" shouts Rudy. "He's okay!" Rudy is thankful JP is thinking and able to hold his head up. He's not sure he could grip the outside of the raft and support JP's head at the same time.

Ben inches his way around the raft, and together they try to pull the raft right side up. It doesn't budge. Another wave bears down on them, and they are carried out of the trough up into the shrieking wind before the wave continues on. Ben notices that most waves are not breaking but just have small curls of white water at the top, and for that he is thankful. If wave after wave were breaking, they would be either free-falling or driven deep underwater every forty to fifty seconds. None of them would be alive within an hour's time.

They try pushing the raft over, but again no luck. Ben and Rudy talk in the trough and decide that if they can all get downwind, perhaps they can work with the blasting gusts to flip the raft back into its proper position. Using the lifeline that encircles the raft, they kick to the downwind side, helping JP as best as they can. They let another wave slip under them, and when they are near the top, where the wind is strongest, Rudy and Ben pull down on the raft, trying to get the opposite end off the water, so the wind can work its way underneath and help finish the job.

The far side of the raft rides up a little bit, as they had hoped, but soon they are back down in the trough, where they are somewhat sheltered from the wind. Again and again they try the technique, but the exhausted men have no luck. They hang on as best they can for a few minutes, until another steep wave breaks on them, as if trying to pound them into submission. They come up coughing and gagging but still have hold of the raft.

Hypothermia will speed its advance, as every part of their bodies is submerged except their heads. They are expending valuable energy just hanging on to the raft's lifeline, craning their necks so they don't breathe in foam or get a mouthful of water. If they stay like this, they won't have to worry about hypothermia—the storm will finish them off by drowning them.

CHAPTER FIFTEEN

MAYDAY ON THE *SEEKER*

For the sailboat *Seeker,* the vessel with the family from Bermuda—husband, wife, and daughter—the past twelve hours have been terrifying. The waves have been so strong that the boat's anchor has been dragging, and now they are in danger of being blown into the roiling water of the Diamond Shoals. The family has held off on calling a Mayday, understanding how dangerous a rescue would be at night, but with some gray dawn light filtering through the rain, they cannot wait any longer. Using the radio, they update SAR Headquarters on their predicament, and all agree that they need to be rescued before it's too late.

Because SAR Headquarters has been in radio communication with the *Seeker* captain and they know the serious nature of the emergency as well as the position, a helicopter is immediately launched from Elizabeth City. This allows the C-130 heading toward the *Sean Seamour II* and *Flying Colours* to continue far out to sea and into the center of the storm.

The helicopter crew is composed of Aircraft Commander Dan Molthen, Copilot Andy Clayton, Rescue Swimmer Mike Ackermann, and Flight Mechanic Dan Cancetty: the same crew that airlifted three men off the fishing boat stranded in the mudflats the prior evening. The crew managed only a couple hours' sleep before the SAR alarm went off for the *Seeker,* and they are operating on adrenaline. They do have a number of factors in their favor: an exact location fix for the vessel, a relatively short flight of about seventy-five miles to the distress scene, and certain radio communication with the captain of the vessel when they arrive.

The ride out is a rough one, with turbulence causing the

helicopter to bounce every which way. Ackermann has flown in high winds, but this is the first time he has ever been airsick. It feels like someone is wringing his stomach. Despite having a good idea how big the seas are below, he can't wait to get on-scene and in the water—both to test his skills and to escape the airsickness.

Copilot Andy Clayton has been flying Jayhawk helicopters for a number of years, but he has been at Elizabeth City only a few months. The seas look awful, and as they descend toward the water near the emergency scene, he is thankful that they have the exact coordinates. Yet when he looks down at the patch of ocean where the *Seeker* should be, he's surprised. The foam and white water from breaking waves stretch in all directions, but there is no sign of the forty-foot sailboat.

Clayton has radio contact with the *Seeker*'s captain, so the pilots know they are in the correct spot, and they descend still lower, to two hundred feet. Suddenly, they spot the boat rising up on the crest of a wave, and the pilots understand why it was so difficult to see. The sailboat is white and blends in with the foam. Using the radio, Clayton begins to explain to the sailors the procedure for the rescue. The boat's captain suggests that they rescue only his wife and daughter; he wants to stay on the vessel to try and save it.

Molthen and Clayton look at each other and shake their heads. If the captain remains on the boat and it capsizes, a second rescue will be infinitely more difficult. And the storm shows no signs of abating. The captain's request does not surprise them; they have heard it many times. Passengers desperately want off the boat before it goes down, while the captain is willing to roll the dice and try to save the vessel. The captain often feels safer and is comforted by the fact that the helicopter found them relatively quickly, and he thinks he can buy more time.

Clayton radios the captain: "Sir, we do not advise that. It's all or nothing. We should take the three of you off now. You are in a dangerous situation. If you want to stay with the boat, the two crew members will have to remain with you, and we do not think that is a wise decision."

After a moment, the captain agrees to follow through with the evacuation. Commander Molthen then lowers the aircraft to a hover of a hundred feet, just off to the side of the *Seeker*. Suddenly a particularly large wave picks up the sailboat and shoves it up toward the helicopter. Molthen reacts by pulling the aircraft up and away from the boat's mast. This addition of power and the lurch skyward remind all four of the crew that the rescue will take every bit of focus.

Now hoist operator Cancetty and rescue swimmer Ackermann are ready to get to work. While the swimmer is being deployed, copilot Clayton is assisting them by calling out the size of the approaching waves. Most waves are an average of thirty feet, but some are almost twice as large, and some are smaller. Cancetty begins lowering Ackermann, trying to time his entry into the ocean to avoid the largest waves. He also wants to get the rescue swimmer in the trough so that he is not in a crest that might drop out from under him. It is important to have the rescue swimmer close to the pitching sailboat, but not so close that the pilots have to worry about another near collision with the boat's mast.

Though the *Seeker* has its anchor in the water, the anchor is dragging as winds pound and push the vessel. Cancetty decides to position the rescue swimmer aft of the vessel so the sailboat will drift back to him. He doesn't want Ackermann expending lots of energy before he begins the rescues.

Cancetty has the best view of the swimmer. The hoist operator wears a gunner's belt with a nylon strap that runs from the belt to a fixed position opposite the doorway, allowing him to lean out the aircraft door and look directly below. He doesn't like what he sees. The waves are so large that the rescue swimmer looks like a speck below. Cancetty can no longer clearly see the swimmer's neon-yellow helmet in the ocean spray, just a tiny body dangling from the cable.

"Forward left," says Cancetty to the pilots through the radio in his helmet. "Now back right. Okay, hold right there."

When Ackermann reaches the water, he releases the cable, and Cancetty immediately starts bringing it back into the helicopter to attach the rescue basket. Ackermann is alone, with no connection to the helicopter, and the seas look like two-story buildings. No amount of training can duplicate these conditions: Swimming pools don't have forty-foot seas or swirling currents. The young rescue swimmer is putting every ounce of his strength in each stroke as he fights the marauding waves to reach the sailboat, which comes in and out of view. He feels like he is swimming uphill and the surface of the hill is rolling at him, like a descending escalator. Wondering if he is making any headway, Ackermann lifts his head from the foam to check on the position of the boat but can see only walls of water. He takes a few more strokes and looks again: still no boat. He looks up at the helicopter. Cancetty is still in the doorway.

Ackermann gets buried by a wave and claws back to the surface. He looks up at Cancetty again, and now he can tell that the hoist operator is pointing. He starts swimming in that direction, knowing that's where the boat is. After a couple more minutes of swimming, he is at the back of the boat, which is pitching up thirty feet and then slamming down by the same amount. He has decided that if he can board the boat, he will do so, to talk to the crew and make sure everyone knows precisely how the rescue will proceed.

If I don't time this perfectly, I'm going to be crushed. Ackermann waits for a wave to slide under him, bringing him even with the vessel. He reaches out and grabs a metal cage on the back of the boat and heaves himself on board. Scrambling to his feet, he lets out a "whew" and is face-to-face with the three sailors. They have blank stares, and Ackermann thinks, *I've never seen people look so gray, at least not anyone alive.* He assumes they have been seasick and awake for well over forty-eight hours.

The first thing the rescue swimmer wants to do is give them confidence that the rescue will go off without a hitch. He doesn't tell them that despite being involved in dozens of SAR cases, he has never seen sea conditions this wild. Instead, he says, "Hey, folks, we're going to get you safe in no time. I do this all the time in these conditions." The father, mother, and daughter stare at him, ashen and shaken. Ackermann has the feeling they are stunned that he actually got through the waves and made it onto their boat. (Commander Molthen later said that Ackermann looked like Spider-Man, climbing up the heaving boat.) Again Ackermann says, "I've been in these conditions plenty of times. You've got nothing to worry about. Now here's what we are going to do . . ."

After briefing the survivors, Ackermann jumps back into the water, upwind of the boat, and motions for the first person—the captain's daughter—to follow him in. He grabs the survivor and looks upward. The basket has blown well aft of the helicopter, and the rescue swimmer watches as the helo moves forward in order to bring the basket closer. When the basket reaches the ocean, Ackermann makes his move and swims the survivor toward it, then assists her inside. He gives the thumbs-up sign to Cancetty.

Cancetty begins the hoist. The winds push the basket one way, and then its weight sends it swinging back the other, careening like a pendulum out of control. As the basket gets closer to the aircraft door, Cancetty leans farther out and wrestles the cable, trying to steady it. When the younger woman reaches the doorway, he pulls her and the basket safely inside and helps her out.

The two pilots are doing their best to keep watch on both the rescue swimmer and the sailboat while they hover at eighty feet. They also keep an eye on the radar altimeter, fluctuating between eighty and forty feet as waves roll under the aircraft. The pilots are relieved there is daylight; they aren't sure a nighttime rescue in such conditions would even be possible.

Cancetty has lowered the hook for Ackermann, and he, too, comes up swinging. When the rescue swimmer reaches the doorway, he uses his arms to push off the helo, and in one motion, he pivots and holds the door handle so that he is facing away from the helo in a sitting position. Cancetty pulls him in back first, like they have done a hundred times in training. The two men quickly discuss the next rescue. They have agreed to try a direct deployment of the rescue swimmer onto the deck of the sailboat. But as Ackermann is being lowered back into the chaos, he decides there is too much motion on the vessel and signals Cancetty to lower him into the ocean. The rescue swimmer then has the next survivor—the captain's wife—jump off the boat, and he repeats the rescue process, getting her safely into the basket.

Because the basket is swinging wildly in the air, the woman is holding the bails (which rise up toward the hook) in a viselike grip. She comes up awkwardly, and when Cancetty pulls her into the helicopter, he has a tough time getting her to release her grip. He pulls on the woman's shoulders, and when that doesn't work, he pries her fingers off the bail one at a time. Then he tilts the basket to make it easier for her to exit. The woman realizes she is safe and rolls out, taking a seat next to her daughter opposite the open doorway.

The third and final deployment and hoist go smoothly. As the captain is brought up in the basket, he extends his arms out to the side of the aircraft to try and steady the basket and assist Cancetty. The hoist operator motions for him to get his arms back inside. It's easy to break an arm if it gets caught between the gyrating basket and the side of the helo.

Once Ackermann is back inside the helicopter, he tries to crawl to the survivors to see if they are okay, but his legs won't move. *Just take deep breaths,* he tells himself. He thinks how ironic it is that just twenty minutes earlier, he wanted so badly to get off the helicopter because of airsickness, and now he is thankful to be back in the chopper. His legs start shaking and spasming uncontrollably, so he lies down on the deck. Mentally, he feels sharp, but physically, he can't move. *And I thought I knew what it was like to give 100 percent . . .*

The pilots make a beeline for Elizabeth City. Ackermann slowly regains feeling in his legs, and he and Cancetty talk with the survivors, making sure they are okay. Ackermann keeps thinking how fortunate they all are. *The ocean gave us just enough opportunity to pull this off. If one thing went differently, we might not be here.* The survivors are exhausted but otherwise in good shape. The sailboat captain puts on a headset and explains to the crew what they went through that night, and the airmen let him know that he was one of four boats in trouble. Cancetty later learns that the survivors are from Bermuda. The flight mechanic explains that he and the crew recently got stuck in Bermuda because of bad weather, and while waiting it out, they enjoyed the local drink, a rum and ginger beer mix called a Dark and Stormy. (A week after the rescue, Cancetty, Molthen, Ackermann, and Clayton receive a large package in the mail. Inside is a case of ginger beer and rum.)

Upon landing, the survivors hug the crew and let them know how grateful they are. When the rotors finally come to a halt, the crew leaves the helo but not the base. Even though they are over their bag limit of flight hours, they are aware of the multiple Maydays and decide to stay on-scene in case they are needed. None of the men have seen a day with so many EPIRBs going off, and they wonder if flying rules might have to be broken in the face of such emergencies.

CHAPTER SIXTEEN

CONVULSIONS

Water pours off Rudy's gray beard. The sixty-two-year-old is being worn down by the effort to hold on to the overturned life raft. But he is also pissed off. It seems he and his mates can't get a break. First the storm behaved differently than forecast; next the GPIRB didn't work properly; and then the life raft got pinned by the spreader. And now the storm seems to have singled them out for punishment by not allowing them to flip the raft right side up. His anger is simmering, and soon it produces adrenaline and strength. Rudy lets go of the lifeline, gets his arms around the top of the inflated tubes, and with a sudden kick from his legs along with a push-up motion from his arms, he gets the upper half of his body onto the overturned raft. He heaves his legs up and collapses facedown on top of the raft. It's a remarkable display of strength, considering he is in waterlogged clothing and foul-weather gear.

Once Rudy catches his breath, he assists Ben in crawling on top. Then the men each grab one of JP's arms and haul him up.

The overturned raft looks like a trampoline, and the three men have to lie prone on it so they don't slip off. They do their best to hide their heads from the wind-driven rain that stings exposed skin, as if someone has taken a handful of gravel and thrown it point-blank into their faces. Ben and Rudy position themselves on either side of JP so he doesn't fall out as the raft rides up and over the giant seas. JP is shaking from the cold, and Ben worries that he won't last another hour. Waves are crashing around them, though fortunately none make a direct hit on the raft. Ben inches closer to JP so that he is almost on top of him, trying to share his body heat and shield him from the wind. A bit of canopy is swaying in the waterlogged raft and

Ben tries to cover JP with it, but there isn't enough of the fabric to do any good.

JP's mind is lucid one moment and foggy the next. He is in the fetal position, his arms and legs tucked in tight, his lips blue. The wind knifes right through his slender frame, and he sadly remembers the survival suits stowed on the boat. They were impossible to access because the broken mast had landed directly on the deck locker the suits were stowed in. The mast was too heavy for the men to lift high enough to open the locker top.

JP knows he is close to the end. He can feel himself convulsing, and the pain from his broken ribs is excruciating. Knowing that losing consciousness from hypothermia will be better than the searing torture caused by his ribs, he waits for the inevitable, even wishing he were back in the water. He thinks of his wife, Mayke, in France and wants to tell her he loves her, and that he's sorry for taking this voyage, that he has done his best.

He tries to talk to Rudy. "Tell Mayke . . ."

Rudy can't understand the rest, but he's sure JP knows he is dying and wants Rudy to pass on a message of love to his wife. Rudy doesn't bother to ask JP to repeat himself. *It's not going to matter,* Rudy thinks, *none of us will be alive to tell anybody anything.*

Rudy looks at JP and tries to hold the captain's head in his arms. JP's entire body convulses twice, then it doesn't move at all. *Is he dead?* wonders Rudy.

Then, pow! A mammoth wave avalanches onto the raft, sending the men into the sea and the raft arching into the air. The churning water engulfs them as if they have gone over a waterfall and are in the vortex below.

Ben and Rudy come up choking, gasping for air. They cannot see JP anywhere. The raft is nearby, and Ben grabs ahold of it. Rudy does the same. The raft is now right side up, but they don't even notice because they are craning their necks, trying to spot JP. Rudy kicks to gain an inch or two of height above the foam, and in the process, he spots JP drifting at least twenty feet away. The Canadian swims to JP, clutches the hood of his friend's foul-weather gear, and drags him back to the raft.

Ben helps Rudy keep a firm grip on JP, and all three men catch their breath. If another wave breaks on the raft, they will lose their hold on it, and the raft will be swept away. Now they notice that the raft is right side up, and this gives them hope. Rudy can see the GPIRB tethered to the middle of the raft, and he thinks, *No wonder the raft was impossible to turn over; the GPIRB was hanging down like an anchor when the raft first flipped.*

JP seems conscious but is staring off into the distance. Rudy shouts, "Hang on! We'll get you back in the raft." JP neither looks at him nor responds. In actuality, JP does hear snatches of Rudy's voice, but it seems miles away. His mind is in a sort of limbo, and he can't feel the pain anymore.

Once again Rudy pulls himself into the raft, and with Ben's help he hoists JP up. Then Ben climbs in, and all three men collapse in a heap, each lost in his own thoughts.

JP feels like he is leaving for somewhere else. His eyes are open, and he looks at the charging combers with wonder. When waves collide, pillars of water shoot high above the seventy-foot mountains, filling the air like geysers. And when they're down in the canyons, JP thinks the sheer walls around him are the most spectacular thing he has ever seen. He feels at peace, ready to go. He's too exhausted and disoriented to think in detail about death, but his acceptance of it is part of his spiritual belief that there is an existential flow to life and perhaps even fate. He is not religious in the traditional sense, but he does believe there is something bigger than all of us, and he hopes there is a continuation of a person's spirit or soul in some way. Yet through this entire emergency, he has never prayed, never asked for help. During the two capsizings, he was in a single-minded problem-solving mode; there was too much to do. Now there is nothing more to be done, and he is letting nature take its course. He is releasing from this earthly life and is surprisingly at peace.

Rudy's spiritual views are similar to JP's in that he keeps an open mind but does not consider any one religion his own. And like JP, he thinks that if there is a God or a higher power, it will not alter the course of events on earth, will not single out one group to help over another. Although Rudy is not a practicing Buddhist, that philosophy appeals to him. He figures he will be dead soon, so he tries to relax, sit back, and enjoy the view. In a sense, Rudy is detaching from the situation and looking at it like an observer. He attempts to measure the waves in increments of ten feet. Starting at the bottom of a trough, he slowly looks up. *Okay, here is the first ten feet, here is the next ten feet.* He continues counting off the sections from the gray liquid wall rising closest to him. When he reaches eighty feet, he is so surprised that he repeats the process, with the same result. *Even if I'm off by ten feet, these waves have got to be at least seventy feet. This is unbelievable, absolutely incredible.* He is fully engaged in the process of observing, almost as if he's at the movie theater, looking at astonishing images flickering on the screen. He starts to take in the sounds, not just the roar of the wind near the wave tops or the crashing of waves that break, but the hissing, snarling noise of the foam passing beneath the raft when they enter a trough. The Gulf Stream is putting on the ultimate show for all the senses, and Rudy knows he is witnessing something only a handful of people on earth have ever seen. This is the definitive battleground, with wind-generated waves coursing into the current of the Stream, where they clash like two enraged titans. And Rudy is on the roller coaster they have created; only at the summit, there is pandemonium, while in the valley, there is relative peace. This ride never stops—it just keeps lifting the men to the point of teetering on a wave top, where the wind lashes their bodies, and then sends them sliding down the combers back side into a relative state of tranquility.

Rudy wonders how long the thin fabric of the raft can hold out against the beating. He figures a few more hours, which is probably longer than they can hang on, considering it has already flipped over twice. Losing the ballast bags, reasons Rudy, makes the raft little better than a child's inflatable pool. Perhaps even worse is that the cover is gone, not just for protection from the wind but for its orange color. Although he doesn't expect to be rescued, he hoped that in a covered raft, a passing ship might find the little vessel and the bodies inside, and at least the families would know they put up a good fight. *I've had a good run,* he says to himself, *I just have to accept this is it.* His mind starts to drift to what will happen after he's gone, what his children will do with his affairs and what their future lives will be like.

Ben is just as calm as the others and tries to think ahead a few hours. *Even if we outlast the storm—which could go on for days—we have no drinking water.* He is aware that hypothermia will likely kill them long before dehydration, but he doesn't feel cold at all. When he was younger, doing his dinghy sailing off the English coast, the temperatures were always cold, so this current exposure doesn't have an impact on him. Still, he knows that their only chance is if the GPIRB transmitted correctly before it went dead.

In a trough, Ben asks Rudy, a trained pilot, "Do you think a helicopter could fly in these conditions?"

Rudy looks out at the crest of the waves, noting how the wind rips spray off their tops, hurling it sideways through the air. "Probably not."

"Didn't think so," says Ben. He wonders if there is anything he can do to help their situation. Bailing would be futile. The flares are useless unless someone is searching for them. But he keeps wondering if he has missed any opportunity to improve their lot, if only to make JP a little more comfortable.

The three men are like soldiers on a battlefield, vastly outnumbered and outgunned, cut off from all help. They know they will be overrun, know they are going to die, but still they defend their little piece of turf, the raft.

PART III

CHAPTER SEVENTEEN

NEED MAX GAS

A ringing telephone wakes up Nevada Smith and his wife at five-thirty a.m. at their home in Camden, North Carolina, about four miles from Air Station Elizabeth City. Nevada, a seasoned Coast Guard helicopter pilot, and his Colombian-born wife, Julieta, are used to such early-morning calls. Julieta answers the phone, then tosses it to Nevada, saying in a soft accent, "It's those Coast Guard guys again."

Nevada sits up and groggily says, "Lieutenant Commander Smith."

On the other end of the line is the operation duty officer (ODO) at Air Station Elizabeth City. "We're having a busy morning. We got some aircraft out right now, and we need another H60 crew. When can you get here? We have a couple EPIRBs going off about 220 nautical miles to the southeast. The Herc [C-130] is on its way right now."

Nevada says, "I'll be there in thirty minutes. I'll need max gas." (Meaning "Add an additional 120-gallon fuel tank and fill all four tanks—three externals and one internal—to maximum capacity, about 6,300 pounds of gas.) A large man at six feet four and 250 pounds, he is now wide awake. "I'm on my way."

Running a hand through his thinning blond hair, he throws on some clothes, then hops in his 1968 Jeep, heading for the air station. He's looking forward to this case because he knows a C-130 will soon be in the vicinity of the distress calls, and that means he will probably be able to focus on the rescue rather than the searching.

Born at the U.S. Naval Air Station in Pensacola, Florida, in 1967, Nevada is the son of a Navy E-2 Hawkeye pilot. It's not surprising

Nevada wanted to fly since he was a little boy, and on every Christmas and birthday, he would ask that his presents include model airplanes. "Over the holidays, I was knocking out model airplanes," recalls Nevada, "like Henry Ford made Model Ts. I had an assembly line going of World War II bombers and fighters." More than thirty airplanes hung from the ceiling of his bedroom, and he started calling it "The Nevada Smithsonian Air Museum." He always got a hoot out of being born in the cradle of naval aviation—Pensacola, Florida, where all Navy, Coast Guard, and Marine Corps pilots start their training. Even his initials are N.A.S., which stands for not only Nevada Allen Smith but also "Naval Air Station."

During his early teen years, Nevada, who was bigger and taller than most of his peers, was encouraged by friends and coaches to play football and basketball. He wasn't interested. Rather than choosing Joe Montana and Julius Erving as his heroes, this teenager idolized pilots: Billy Mitchell, Pappy Boyington, Paul Tibbets, the Wright Brothers, Chuck Yeager, and his father and all his dad's ex-navy flying buddies. He wanted to be like those guys.

Upon graduating from high school, Nevada went to college at Southern Illinois University at Edwardsville and joined the U.S. Air Force ROTC program. His dream of the air force, however, was short-lived: He was half an inch too tall to properly fit in the cockpit of a fighter jet. It was a disappointment, but not devastating, because Nevada, then nineteen, could still fly for the seagoing services—the navy, the marines, or the Coast Guard. He transferred to Iowa State and spent another year in Navy ROTC. The out-of-state tuition was quite high, and his dad offered him an alternative: If Nevada transferred to college in Carbondale, Illinois, he could use the savings to pay for flight lessons.

After securing his pilot's license, Nevada spent much of his free time reading about pilots and aircraft. While looking through an aviation magazine, he read an article about the new HH-60J Jayhawks that the Coast Guard would soon add to its inventory. His eyes lingered on a picture of an H-60 medium-range helicopter used by the Coast Guard for search and rescue. It was love at first sight.

Prior to his graduation from college, he applied to the Coast Guard's officer candidate school (OCS) but was rejected. This time he was devastated. Then he thought, *That's not going to stop me, I'll enlist!* He was living in the small town of Roscoe, Illinois, a few miles south of the Wisconsin border, about two hours from Chicago. He told his mother he was driving to the Coast Guard's recruiting office in Chicago. "Don't sign anything," said his mother, "until you talk to your father."

Nevada went to Chicago and signed every form the recruiter put in front of him. He took his Armed Services Vocational Aptitude Battery Test in a run-down brick building in Rockford, Illinois. After the test, he got in his car and heard that the bombing of Baghdad had started. He was off to boot camp in Cape May, New Jersey, just a few weeks later—February 1991, during the Gulf War.

Upon graduation from boot camp, Nevada was turned down a second time for OCS. Instead, he did a tour on a buoy tender on the Mississippi River. After that assignment, he once again tried to gain entry into OCS, and this time he was accepted. His good fortune continued when the Coast Guard sent him to the extremely demanding navy flight school in Pensacola, Florida. He earned his wings of gold in 1995, and his father pinned the same wings on his son that he had earned twenty-six years earlier. Over the next few years, Nevada flew on dozens of SAR missions, including rescuing victims of Hurricane Katrina. In 2005 he auditioned for the movie *The Guardian* and landed the role of Lieutenant Ken Krauss. It was an exciting time for the young pilot: He spent two weeks filming in Shreveport, Louisiana, followed by two days in Elizabeth City and one in Hollywood.

Now, arriving at Air Station Elizabeth City, Nevada is thinking that today's SAR mission will be relatively routine. It's raining, with wind gusts up to thirty knots—the usual nasty weather he flies in. He parks his Jeep, runs into the Operations Center, dons his flight suit, and quickly talks to the watch captain, Tom Romero, who informs him that he will be the aircraft commander, and his copilot will be Aaron Nelson.

Normally, in the lower forty-eight the commander takes the right seat to monitor the hoist, but Nevada knows Aaron is an amazing pilot and decides he will be in the right seat and Nevada in the left. Although Aaron has been in the Coast Guard only three years, he has more flying experience than Nevada. The thirty-five-year-old pilot grew up in North Dakota, but unlike Nevada, he didn't make flying a career goal until his junior year of high school. His guidance counselor noticed he wasn't applying himself to his studies, yet he still was a B student. The counselor asked what he wanted to do with his life. Aaron hadn't given it much thought, but because his brother was in the air force, he said, "I'd like to fly planes." The counselor said he might be able to help, and he walked Aaron through the steps necessary to get into the Air Force Academy. "You need to get in shape," said the counselor, "and have a near-perfect GPA. Start taking tougher courses, like physics."

This challenge was exactly what Aaron needed, and with a new sense of purpose, he began to exercise daily and earn straight As. A friend offered further motivation when he started taking flying lessons and invited Aaron to come along. Aaron sat in the backseat and watched his friend and the instructor go through the preflight checklist. When the plane zipped down the runway and was airborne, Aaron blurted out, "This is the coolest thing. I want to fly one of these." He soon found a part-time job and used the income for his own flight lessons, getting his pilot's license about the time he graduated from high school. His goal to go to the Air Force Academy was derailed when he was rejected, apparently because of the B average prior to his junior year.

Aaron's father pointed out another path, saying the army used warrant officer pilots. "What's that?" asked Aaron. "I don't know exactly," was his father's response, "but warrant officers are experts at their jobs, and as pilots, all they do is fly—which is what you want to do." Within a week Aaron was talking to army recruiters about the warrant officer flight training program. Since Aaron didn't have a college degree, the recruiters set the bar high, saying, "You not only have to pass all the tests, you have to score above average." Aaron did well on the tests, and a few months later, he went through basic training and then on to U.S. Army flight school at the age of nineteen. Upon graduation, he was stationed in Germany, then Hawaii, flying primarily Black Hawk helicopters. After eight years, Aaron left the active-duty army and flew for two commercial airlines while continuing to fly Black Hawk helicopters part-time in the Hawaii

Army National Guard. In 2004, now married with children, Aaron was concerned about the downturn in business at his airline and decided to take a more secure flying position with the Coast Guard, and was assigned to Elizabeth City. He was often teamed with Nevada Smith, and the two men worked well together. Now, on the morning of May 7, 2007, they were headed out for yet another mission.

While the two pilots are being briefed in the Operations Center, they are joined by Flight Mechanic Scott Higgins and Aviation Survival Technician (rescue swimmer) Drew Dazzo. Nevada is glad to see both men; he now has a very experienced crew. The four men about to launch in the Jayhawk all had the night off and were called in as backup because the on-duty crew had already launched for the *Seeker*.

Nevada conducts a prebrief with his team, explaining that two sailboats have activated their EPIRBs about 220 nautical miles out to sea off Cherry Point, North Carolina. They have little other information to go on because the C-130 has yet to make radio contact with those in distress. Reports coming back from the C-130 describe how the wind gusts are getting higher and higher as they approach the emergency. This mission that Nevada thought would be routine is beginning to look quite challenging. He and his crew assume the offshore seas are extreme for two boats to have activated their EPIRBs, but none of the men imagine they are going into a storm with winds over hurricane force.

"Make sure we have the external fuel tank on," says Nevada to Scott, "and max fuel." Both men know the HH-60 Jayhawk might need every drop of fuel going so far offshore to multiple EPIRBs with little concrete information. Scott, like Nevada, is thankful that each member of the crew has been around long enough to have participated in all sorts of SARs and flown into just about every kind of weather the Atlantic can stir up. He, Nevada Smith, and Drew Dazzo have been three of the select few sent to advanced rescue swimmer school, practicing rescues in heavy seas at the Columbia River Bar off the coast of Oregon, where every decision and action must be made at warp speed because of the turbulent conditions.

Scott feels at somewhat of a disadvantage because they have so little information to go on. Normally, he tries to glean every fact from the prebriefing that will help him, such as the heading of the vessel in distress, its speed, and the condition of survivors. He especially wants to know whether the people in distress are ambulatory; that can influence his decision to use a basket or a litter, which is larger and more difficult to maneuver. He wants to be prepared so that when he arrives on-scene, he will have gone over the rescue plans with Drew. On this case, they have no idea what to expect and little information about the sea state so far offshore.

When he got the call at home, Scott thought that it was just another false alarm. Outside his bedroom window, only a light breeze was blowing. In his twelve years with the Coast Guard, 80 percent of the SAR cases he flew on turned out to be false alarms or hoaxes—usually some kid calling Mayday on Channel 13 or someone shooting a flare from a boat, perhaps not realizing that it is the international symbol of distress.

The four crewmen gather outside on the tarmac at their helicopter. Nevada yells to Scott, "I'll be in the left seat, running things. Lieutenant Nelson will be in the right seat, so he'll be working with you on the hoists. He's a better pilot than I am, anyway." Scott nods, and then each man gives the helicopter a once-over to make sure everything is in order and nothing is missing. Scott and Drew check inside the cabin for the rescue equipment, in place along with the medical supplies. Drew is the flight's emergency medical technician, and it will be his job to stabilize and assist any injured survivors.

The HH-60 Jayhawk is almost like home to the crew. They have spent so much time training in the fourteen-thousand-pound helicopter that they can find every instrument, lever, door, and cable with their eyes closed. Stations such as Cape Cod, Kodiak, Mobile, and Elizabeth City have the HH-60 for offshore rescue, while other stations have the smaller and shorter-range Dolphin helicopter. The Jayhawk is a large aircraft, at seventeen feet in height and sixty-five feet in length, and its four main rotors have a diameter of fifty-four feet. It is powered by two General Electric gas turbine engines that can propel it at speeds of up to 170 knots, although the helicopter cruises best at 140 knots. The cockpit contains what seems, to the nonaviation observer, an almost overwhelming number of instruments and switches. The pilots monitor their instruments to be sure the helicopter's systems are performing properly, but they also scan the horizon for other aircraft, boats, and the sea state. Fortunately, the cockpit has windows in the front, at foot level, on the sides, and even above. The helicopter also has the latest satellite-aided navigation system, as well as radar mounted in its nose to assist in searching. A video camera mounted on the underbelly of the aircraft can project a picture on a monitor in front of the pilots so they can see a small partial area beneath them. But the camera can't paint the image that the hoist operator is able to give the pilots of what is happening in the water below, particularly in regard to the cable and the rescue swimmer. The cable itself is two hundred feet long and surprisingly thin, about the size of your pinkie finger. It is composed of dozens of woven steel strands, which give it the strength to hoist up to eleven thousand pounds of weight; the basket, however, is rated for six hundred pounds. As tough as the cable is, the strands can fray if it rubs up against any part of the helicopter. If this happens, the real danger is not that the cable will break but that it will start to unravel and get stuck in the spool. This situation, called "birdcaging," means that the rescue swimmer and a survivor can get stuck halfway between the helo and the water, or left in the water with no way to extract them.

Depending on weather conditions and wind direction, the Jayhawk's fuel can fly a crew of four roughly three hundred miles out to sea, conduct a rescue of forty-five minutes, and have enough gas left in the tanks to return to land. Nevada wants max fuel because he doesn't know how long it will take to locate the vessel or people in the water; nor does he know the wave heights that will play a role in how long Drew might have to be in the ocean. He's also thinking about the second EPIRB and wondering whether he'll be able to do two rescues in the same area.

One of the primary instruments Nevada and Aaron will monitor at the rescue site is the radar altimeter. The pilots need to keep the aircraft low enough that Scott can manage the cable and get Drew as close as possible to the survivors, but high enough that it doesn't get hit by a wave. If enough water hits the engines, they will "flame out," and the helo will drop like a stone. When it hits the sea, it doesn't stay upright but, rather, "turtles." The large heavy rotors pull the body of the aircraft to one side or the other, and the helicopter quickly goes upside down. That is why all four crew members have completed a grueling water course with a simulator, meant to train them to exit an aircraft in the water. The simulator is called the "Dunker," and the crew is strapped into their seats wearing blacked-out goggles and full flight suits. The Dunker is dropped into a swimming pool and rolled upside down, and the crew has to escape. They learn to orient themselves, use handholds to feel their way out, and if necessary, grab a small amount of air from a tiny oxygen tank called a helicopter emergency egress device (HEED). They also practice without the HEED by simply holding their breath, trying to stay calm, and feeling their way out of a door or pushing out a window. More than one airman has had reoccurring nightmares from this most harrowing form of training. Yet if a real crash occurs, this is exactly the hellish situation they will be in, only a heck of a lot more violent.

The threat of such a scenario is very real and has happened more than once in the last ten years. One of the more publicized cases was the December 2004 crash of a Jayhawk off the coast of Unalaska Island, Alaska, during a rescue. The Jayhawk was sent to a sinking cargo ship, the *Selendang Ayu,* and was in the process of airlifting the crew. The rescue swimmer had been deployed directly to the cargo ship; six sailors were safely hoisted to the helicopter, and a seventh was being brought up in the basket when disaster struck. A rogue wave caught the pilots unaware and engulfed the helicopter in spray and water, causing the engine to stall, which sent the helo tumbling down, where it clipped the side of the ship and fell into the sea. The three-man helicopter crew all managed to extricate themselves from the wreck and, with the aid of their survival suits, stayed alive until a Coast Guard crew flying a Dolphin rescued them and the one survivor being hoisted at the time of the crash. The six sailors who had been airlifted into the Jayhawk perished. The rescue swimmer and the ship's captain were still on board the cargo ship, and the seas tore that in two before the crew on the Dolphin rescued them.

This crash illustrates the dangers of a low-altitude hover during a rescue. The longer a helicopter stays close to the ocean during a storm, the greater are the odds that it will encounter a freak wave.

NOAA meteorologists estimate that one out of every thousand waves will be *double* the height of the average seas. Add a sailing vessel's tall mast into the mix, and the danger increases twofold. It's for this reason that the pilots and hoist operator monitor not only the rescue swimmer but also any approaching waves that look larger than the ones already encountered.

The hoisting cable dangling from the aircraft poses its own set of perils. In Hawaii, a Dolphin helicopter crew was performing practice hoist operations with a forty-seven-foot Coast Guard motor lifeboat when its cable tangled with the boat's dewatering standpipe. The tension on the cable caused it to snap and hit the helicopter's main rotor. The Dolphin crew immediately started to fly toward a safe landing area but got only two miles before incurring a catastrophic rotor failure that sent the helicopter plummeting 450 feet into the sea. None of the four crewmen survived.

In an accident in April 2010, a crew of three did survive a harrowing nighttime crash, in part because of their training in the Dunker. In this case, the Dolphin did not drop out of the sky, but the crew became disoriented in the darkness, and the aircraft's nose struck the water while flying over Lake Huron. Lieutenant Tasha Hood was the copilot that night; she, the aircraft commander, and the flight mechanic were conducting a routine training flight in which they practiced lowering and hoisting the rescue basket to and from a forty-one-foot Coast Guard small boat. Tasha recalls that there was no moonlight or starlight, so that even with night vision goggles, the horizon was nearly impossible to distinguish. During the hoist, the boat's masthead light provided the pilots and flight mechanic with their only visual reference while they completed three underway boat hoists. They were operating just thirty feet above the water, and the pilot used the helicopter's hover augmentation mode to help hold the aircraft's altitude in the challenging environment. During the transition to forward flight, disaster struck. The pilot had completed the last hoist and started to air-taxi away from the illuminated hoisting platform into complete darkness. The flight mechanic was in the process of stowing the rescue basket while Tasha disengaged the augmentation mode and made a radio call to the small boat. The total darkness caused the pilot to experience spatial disorientation, and instead of climbing forward and away from the boat, the aircraft was flying at a slight descent. Before either pilot regained situational awareness from the cockpit instruments, the helicopter hit the water nose-first, and its tail flipped right over it, just like when a boat pitchpoles.

"It happened so suddenly," says Tasha, "that I just remember thinking, *I'm upside down underwater, and it's dark.*" That was when her training kicked in. She had been taught to count to eight, as per the emergency procedure, before trying to exit the aircraft to avoid injury by moving rotors or a running engine. She made it to six, then tried to release her five-point harness. It would not come free. Instead of her life flashing before her eyes, she saw a headline that read "Copilot Dies Strangled in Harness in Coast Guard Helicopter Crash." Her Dunker training kept her from full-blown panic. She paused and tried the harness again. This time it came free. Her left hand found the hose to her oxygen tank while she used her right hand to reach across her chest and grab the airframe. "At this moment, I realized I was running out of air. Each second felt like an eternity in the darkness." The aircraft's doors had been ripped off in the crash, as well as the entire glass bubble (windshield) enclosing the cockpit. Tasha moved to her left and noticed that the dry suit she was wearing was naturally buoyant and was pulling her free of the aircraft. She decided to go in the direction the dry suit was tugging her, and she made it to the surface without having to use her small oxygen apparatus, which would have been difficult, submerged and upside down.

She at first thought she was in an air bubble in the cockpit, but as her eyes adjusted, she realized she had surfaced next to the helo's landing gear in one-foot waves. She screamed for the pilot and flight mechanic, wondering how she would be able to dive back down in the buoyant dry suit to try and free them. Then she saw their helmets bobbing in the water—both men had found their way out of the helicopter and were floating in the 50-degree water. During the crash, the flight mechanic's dry suit had ripped, and he was feeling the effects of the encroaching cold water tugging down on him. He inflated his life vest, and Tasha did the same and then went to him, and they linked arms. Fortunately, the utility boat was not far away, and the crewmen were rescued in just ten minutes.

Incredibly, the crew suffered only minor injuries; Tasha was especially lucky because her helmet flew off when the helo slammed into the water.

Tasha was back flying in three weeks, thankful for her Dunker training. She now realizes that when she was upside down, it was probably her weight on the safety harness that made it difficult to unlock. Today when she flies, she makes certain she knows the exact location of her vest knife, should she need to cut her way out of the harness. "And I will never complain about wearing a dry suit again. It pulled me to the surface and kept me there."

All four of the crewmen flying out to the *Sean Seamour II* are dressed in the same fire-retardant dry suits that helped save Tasha Hood's life. A dry suit is required whenever crew members operate over waters colder than 70 degrees. If they crash into the water, these suits have seals at the end of the arms and legs to help the crew fight off hypothermia. Though the suits do breathe a bit, they can make the men uncomfortably hot while flying, especially if they pick up hypothermic survivors who need the helo's heater at its maximum temperature. Drew and Scott, who will be doing the most physical kind of work, will feel like they are in a sauna if they need to blast the heater for chilled survivors.

The suits are bright orange, except for the one worn by Scott Higgins, whose green flight suit is an indication of his other duties as an aerial gunner precision marksman. The thirty-three-year-old six-footer with black hair is somewhat unusual in that he wears these two hats and does extensive training for very different purposes. His role as flight engineer/hoist operator is to save lives, while his role as a marksman is to take out anyone who threatens the lives of American citizens or elected officials.

Scott's first tour of duty was at Air Station Cape Cod, where he learned all about the Jayhawk and its systems while also practicing hoist operations with rescue swimmers and, finally, participating in actual SARs. His next assignment was Clearwater, Florida, where he was stationed for two years before being assigned to the elite Maritime Security Response Team air wing. He was sent to Mobile, Alabama, and received special weapons training along with such tactics as vertical insertion (also called fast roping) and firing rifles from helicopters. After a few months he was transferred to Elizabeth City, where he continued his dual role as precision marksman and flight mechanic. Elizabeth City offered more than its share of SARs, and one case he'll never forget was a New Year's Eve emergency, when his helo crew responded to a sinking boat being shredded by churning surf in an area of shoals. From his perch in the helicopter, Scott could see that the boat was half submerged, so he immediately lowered the rescue swimmer before the vessel went down and the captain was swept away. To expedite the rescue, the pilot, Dan Molthen, Scott, and the rescue swimmer, Mike Lineahan, decided to use the strop (a simple sling) rather than the rescue basket. The rescue swimmer was dangling about five feet above the surf off to the starboard side of the boat, signaling for the man to jump off the pitching vessel so that a water rescue could be performed. The captain was paralyzed with fear and would not jump. Minutes went by, with the pilots holding the helo in a hover, while Scott adjusted the cable to keep the swimmer above the surf, and the swimmer frantically motioned for the man to get in the water. Finally, after four minutes of coaxing, the captain leaped into the churning seas, and the rescue swimmer released from the strop and swam to the survivor. It should have been a quick hoist, but the captain, who was much larger than the rescue swimmer, panicked again. He thought he was drowning and started grabbing and hugging the rescue swimmer rather than relaxing and letting himself be helped. Scott watched in alarm as the two men were rolled by a wave. When they surfaced, the captain was clawing at the rescue swimmer's mask and snorkel. This is where the rescue swimmer's years of training paid off. Even though he was smaller than the petrified captain, he was able to get the upper hand and slide the strop around him, and soon they were lifted up together.

Situations like that taught Scott to expect the unexpected. And now, as he and his fellow crew members launch for the long flight to the *Sean Seamour II,* he starts playing different scenarios in his mind, reminding himself that there is nothing routine when a rescue is this far offshore.

CHAPTER EIGHTEEN

TETHER OURSELVES TOGETHER

Drowning and hypothermia are the first two obstacles that JP, Rudy, and Ben will have to overcome to stay alive through the day, but not far off will be two new challenges: sharks and dehydration. With the surface of the ocean in such a chaotic state, sharks in the area are probably staying well below the crashing waves. But as soon as the seas abate, the life raft will attract them like a magnet. In a section of ocean devoid of floating objects, a life raft is a curiosity for sharks, and they will come and investigate. Colors also draw sharks, and bright colors in particular are a focus, while dark hues such as deep blue and black are the least appealing. So while life rafts need to be a bright color for planes, helicopters, and boats to spot, those same colors are increasing the odds of the life raft being visited by sharks. The bottom part of JP's life raft—all that is left—is black, but a couple of tattered slices of the orange canopy trail off its side.

Because sharks can sense vibrations in the water, a person moving or bailing inside the life raft is sending out a signal to sharks that seems to say, "Come here, there is something alive and wounded." Large sharks, such as blues, mako, and great whites, fear nothing and are lured in by the sounds and motion and, eventually, the sight of something large and unusual in the ocean. A shark often finds a meal in the form of other fish swimming beneath the raft. Maybe it's the shade provided by the raft or its color or structure to hide behind, but bait fish will fin beneath it, which in turn attracts larger fish, and those will get the attention of sharks. And once the sharks linger, they are sure to know that something is alive inside it.

Curiously, instead of attacking the raft with their teeth, most sharks, upon first encountering a raft, "bump" the vessel. These

117

bumps can be in the form of a gentle nudge or a rubbing of the shark's back along the entire length of the raft. Perhaps sharks use bumping as a cautious way to probe the raft to sense what is inside, or, with harder blows, to knock its contents into the sea. The bumps and blows escalate into attacks if there is more than a single shark at the raft or if a shark sees there is a living creature—food—inside the raft. Laura Hillenbrand, in her book *Unbroken,* describes how Louis Zamparini and two other castaways in a life raft were being circled and nudged by sharks until Louie leaned over the edge of the raft. One of the sharks "leapt from the water at a terrific speed, mouth wide open, lunging straight at his head." Louie lifted his hands in front of his face and managed to turn the shark just before it took his head in its mouth. Later in his ordeal, Louie encountered a different kind of assault by a shark, this one by a twenty-foot great white that sped up from the depths, crashed into the raft, and sent it airborne. Somehow all three castaways managed to stay inside, so the shark tried knocking them out with its tail. It was only after several harrowing tail slaps against the raft that the shark glided away. A similar experience happened to Bill and Simonne Butler, husband and wife, who drifted in the Pacific in a leaky life raft after their boat was sunk by a pod of pilot whales. In Bill's book, *66 Days Adrift,* he describes how medium-sized sharks "punched, shoved, and knocked" their raft throughout an entire night, causing him to wonder how much punishment the raft could take. The raft was tested by sharks—perhaps the same ones—many more nights, but Bill and Simonne were able to patch small leaks, keeping it afloat. A new problem occurred when the sharks left. Bill caught some fish to eat and threw the carcasses overboard, where triggerfish ate them. A few minutes later, Bill wondered why the triggerfish scattered when he threw fish guts into the sea. He peered into the ocean and learned why: "A great white shark with a head two feet in diameter" was under the raft. The great white stayed with the raft for the entire day, and as nightfall closed in, the raft was violently spun around 180 degrees. Bill feared it was the great white, but as he squinted into the dusk, he was "met with one of the happiest sights I have ever seen." A group of smaller sharks was attacking the raft, which meant the great white had moved on.

* * *

For now JP, Rudy, and Ben keep their worries about sharks in check, knowing that first the raft must stay in one piece throughout the storm. They have no idea how long the unnamed storm will last, but already they are moderately thirsty and rue the fact that the survival bag is at the bottom of the ocean instead of in the raft. All three men have been expending energy fighting the sea, and even when they are not moving, they are losing internal water through the vapor they exhale just by breathing. JP, in particular, did so many tasks and put forth so much effort on the *Sean Seamour II* that he should have been hydrating himself frequently before he abandoned ship. But there was so much happening, so many decisions, and so much pain from the broken ribs, that drinking water was the last thing on his mind. Now there is no fresh water, and sipping seawater, even a few drops, is out of the question. The sodium in salt water must be removed by urinating, which causes the loss of even more fluid. And drinking larger amounts of seawater will lead to death, as it pulls moisture out of brain cells, leading to hallucinations while increasing the rate of dehydration.

JP will be the first of the three to feel the effects of dehydration, because he is already suffering from hypothermia and shock. Indeed, mild dehydration may have played a role in the convulsions he suffered earlier. The effects of initial dehydration include light-headedness, lethargy, muscle cramps, and confusion. As the dehydration worsens, it can lead to seizures, palpitations, and eventual unconsciousness. A dehydrated person's blood vessels will constrict to compensate for the loss of fluid in the blood in order to maintain blood pressure for vital organs. The reaction is similar to what happens with hypothermia, where blood is restricted to the outer extremities so that vital organs can function. Because JP is suffering from both problems, he is getting a double dose of trouble. He needs to get warm and hydrated, fast.

JP continues to come in and out of consciousness. He has watched the near vertical walls of water assault the raft and thinks that the storm will last a lot longer than he can hang on. He thinks of Rudy's age—sixty-two—and knows that his odds of survival aren't much better. Maybe Ben, only thirty-one, will have the stamina to outlast the storm and stay alive long enough to be found. That is a long shot, and JP knows it, so he tugs on Rudy's raingear and says, "Maybe we should all tether ourselves together."

Rudy and Ben are surprised to hear JP talk, but they understand what he is saying. They know he means that if they tether themselves to one another and then to the raft, their bodies will have a better chance of being found.

"I was thinking the same thing," says Rudy, his voice trailing off. He knows it will be easier on the families if their bodies are recovered.

As the Jayhawk launches, Commander Nevada Smith, Copilot Aaron Nelson, Rescue Swimmer Drew Dazzo, and Flight Mechanic Scott Higgins settle in for the 250-mile flight, which will take about an hour and forty-five minutes. The first hundred miles are rough, but nothing Scott hasn't flown through in the past. They are cruising between five and nine hundred feet above the ocean, through rain and wind gusts of forty-five knots. Visibility is between a quarter to a half mile, and the flight is below cloud cover. It's hard to judge the height of the waves at this altitude, without any boats or structure in the water for contrast, but Scott guesses they are about twenty feet. "Shouldn't be too bad," he says to Drew over the radio in their headsets.

The rescue swimmer nods and says, "It'll be just like advanced rescue school."

Drew is also keeping an eye on the waves below, and though he guesses they are fifteen to twenty feet, he notes the amount of white water and figures that the interval between waves is short and that each wave is steep enough to be breaking. He is also listening to Nevada and Aaron on the radio, keeping everyone apprised of the climbing wind speeds. "We've got gusts of fifty," says Nevada. A few minutes later, "Gusts have climbed to sixty." The helicopter is being bumped and buffeted, making the ride uncomfortable, and they are far from the storm's center. Sometimes it gets pushed from side to side; sometimes it drops and rises abruptly. The pilots begin to alter course slightly whenever they encounter the most severe squalls.

Drew hears the C-130 commander over the radio, giving them directions on the best altitudes. He also hears them calling out wind gusts of eighty knots. *Holy shit,* he thinks, *that's unbelievable.* Being a swimmer, he tries to imagine the state of the ocean in the face of such winds. He doesn't like the picture beginning to form.

Despite the fact that the C-130 is reporting such dangerous wind speeds, Drew is comforted to hear the voice of the airplane's commander. If the C-130 crew can spot the boat in trouble or the people in the water, Drew knows he can get right to work without having to wait through the search part of the SAR. He also knows he will have another set of eyes looking down on him when he begins the rescue. The C-130 crew members are his angels, men and women who look after him if something goes wrong on the helicopter. They won't be able to extract him from the ocean, but they will be above him with the ability to drop survival equipment, and that is reassuring when treading water alone far out to sea.

Drew is getting himself psyched for the rescue, as an athlete would before a big game. He's got the butterflies in the stomach that he always gets when he knows the conditions are bad. It's a feeling he relishes; it means his adrenaline is on standby. He's got a hunch that this rescue will be one of his more difficult, and he quickly runs through trouble he might expect, recalling other SARs he performed. The thirty-four-year-old has been in the Coast Guard for eight years, and unlike some of his peers, he did not dream of being a rescue swimmer; he chose the career path after trying other work.

Drew grew up in Ridge, Long Island, and was one of those kids who could never sit still. He always wanted to be outside doing something—racing BMX bicycles and dirt bikes, along with playing soccer, hockey, and volleyball. Although he was never on his high school swim team, he spent a lot of time on the ocean, using a small family boat for fishing trips and waterskiing. After he finished high school, he wasn't sure what he wanted to do, so he took the first job offered to him, as a carpenter hired to frame houses. He swung a hammer for the next several years until, when he was twenty-five, he and his parents visited the U.S.S. *Intrepid* museum in New York City. The Coast Guard was also there, putting on a demonstration off the stern of the aircraft carrier. Drew watched with fascination as a boat dropped someone in the water, then a helicopter swooped in and a rescue swimmer leaped out and went through a mock rescue. Right then and there, Drew had an epiphany and turned to his father and said, "I want to be that rescue swimmer." He finally knew what he wanted to do with his life, though reaching his goal would take a lot more than desire and hard work. It would require a single-minded, all-consuming quest and a real gut check of his mental and physical stamina.

First he went to the Coast Guard recruiting office and passed the physical. His background check turned up a DUI, and the recruiter told him that the black mark on his record might be insurmountable. Drew wrote a series of essays about why he would be a good addition to the Coast Guard, but they weren't enough. He added recommendations from all the adults who knew him, along with a letter from his congressman. Finally, just after his twenty-sixth birthday, Drew began his three months of boot camp in Cape May. Upon completion, the Coast Guard allowed each new member to request where they would like to be stationed. Drew wanted to get as far away from New York as possible and be close to a wilderness area, so on his selection sheet, he wrote, "Anywhere in Alaska."

The Coast Guard was happy to oblige. Drew was sent to Sitka, where he was a fireman on a buoy tender. As soon as he achieved the required six months of service, he submitted his name for rescue swimmer school. Only a handful of hopeful candidates get accepted, and of those who do, only a small percent graduate. (There are only about three hundred rescue swimmers in the entire Coast Guard.) Drew had an eighteen-month wait in Sitka before he was allowed to compete for one of the coveted rescue swimmer positions, formally known as aviation survival technician. During that time, his life and responsibilities changed significantly from his days as a carefree house framer. He fell in love, married, and became a stepfather to his wife's daughter from a previous marriage.

When Drew finally began the first phase of his quest to become a rescue swimmer, he was, at twenty-eight, one of the older candidates. He initially went through the rigors of the four-month aviation survival technician (AST) training program, and then it was on to another four months of training at AST A-School, held at Elizabeth City. (Only about seventy-five candidates are accepted to the school, and the training is on par with the difficulty of what Army Rangers, Navy SEALs, and air force pararescue jumpers must endure.) At A-School, instructors want to see how candidates respond in various water drills under stressful situations. The goal is to push the trainees to their limits and beyond so that only the most committed men or women are left. (Women undergo the same training and tests as men; there are currently three active female rescue swimmers.) About half the trainees wash out of this part of the program. Those who make it are then sent to emergency medical technician training school, and upon successful completion, they are admitted into the apprentice program at one of the Coast Guard air stations.

Like all the other candidates, Drew found the process extremely demanding, but he had a slight advantage over some of the other trainees, because prior to being admitted to the program, he put himself on a grueling daily exercise regimen so he could be as prepared as possible. He knew that only the Coasties in great physical shape sign up to become rescue swimmers, and he also was aware the instructors would drive them all to the breaking point. Drew needed to be his strongest and fastest, but also to develop a stamina that few people have. While all that preparation helped, A-School required him to dig much deeper and draw on a mental toughness he wasn't aware he had.

The water drills, particularly the buddy swim and the "bullpen" session, challenged Drew's endurance. In the buddy swim, he had to drag a person eight hundred meters without stopping to rest. The bullpen session was even worse. Six instructors encircle the rescue swimmer and, one at a time, act like a panicked, drowning person, tugging, hugging, clawing, and pulling the rescue swimmer down. The swimmer must somehow break their grip without punching them in the head while still getting enough air to keep from drowning. Drew was able to perform better than most of the candidates in these water drills, but he found the long-distance runs to be a real gut check. Equally tough was being away from his wife and daughter for several months.

Upon Drew's graduation, he was fortunate to be stationed in Hawaii, and it was here that he performed his first rescue: saving his own daughter. He and his family were at the beach when his daughter, at age six, got caught in a rip current. "Daddy, Daddy!" she screamed. Drew went after her, and by the time he caught up, they were seventy-five yards out. He said, "Everything's going to be okay. Just ride on my back." He then did the breaststroke, going parallel to the shore. He could feel the pull of the rip, and he kept as much of his body near the surface as possible because rip tides are stronger deep down. After about five minutes, he felt the current release them, and he was able to head in.

The rescue meant the world to Drew. There was no helicopter, no free-fall jump, and no hoist, but his daughter was safe, and Drew knew it was because of his training.

For the four and a half years that Drew was in Hawaii, the water rescue of his daughter turned out to be the only one he performed. He had plenty of medevacs of injured people off vessels, but not the water rescues he trained so hard for. He even began hoping the SAR alarm would send out its piercing warble so he could be dropped into the ocean.

His next station assignment was Elizabeth City, and he decided to stop obsessing about water rescues. As soon as he stopped thinking about it, the cases started coming in whenever he was on duty. His fellow rescue swimmers began to notice. The swimmers are a tight-knit group, and they have their own "shop" where one of them is always stationed by a phone, radio, or computer to monitor any potential SARs. The other swimmers are either working out or organizing rescue equipment, from dry suits to parachutes to life rafts. Hanging on the walls of the equipment room up near the ceiling are life vests worn by the people saved by the rescue swimmers. Written on each PFD in Magic Marker is the name of the survivor, the vessel, the date of the rescue, and the name of the swimmer. Drew's name was starting to appear on several PFDs, and the newer swimmers would say, "Why is it you're getting so many rescues?" Drew would smile and say, "Good things happen to those who wait." Then he would explain that except for saving his daughter in Hawaii, he didn't have a single water rescue in his four years there.

And now Drew is flying over two hundred miles out to sea for yet another SAR, and he thinks, *I'm not even supposed to be the backup rescue swimmer.* The day before, a fellow rescue swimmer had been incarcerated in the county jail after getting into an altercation at a bar. Drew spent much of the day figuring out the legal process of getting his friend released and working with a bail bondsman. The arrested rescue swimmer was scheduled to stand duty as a backup swimmer that night, but a superior didn't think it was a good idea. So Drew volunteered to be the backup. That night he tuned in to the TV weather report and heard about the potential for high winds. He wasn't surprised when, a few hours later, the phone rang at five a.m. and he was told that the on-duty swimmer had been sent to the *Seeker* and Drew was needed at the station ASAP.

Drew gazes out the window of the helo, then looks at Scott, who has been doing the same. It's hard to tell, but the waves now look to be forty feet. Both men have done all sorts of difficult water rescues, but neither has done one in seas this large. And they still have another half hour of flying southeast into the storm, into the Gulf Stream.

CHAPTER NINETEEN

"MARK, MARK, MARK!"

It is seven a.m., and the C-130 is below cloud cover, being buffeted and blasted by eighty-knot winds. Copilot Edward Ahlstrand sits next to Aircraft Commander Paul Beavis, and both are in absolute awe of what they see below. Ahlstrand knows he is witnessing waves of a magnitude he will never see again. He expected bad conditions, but this is something else entirely. Even the color of the ocean is different than anything he's encountered. There is an absence of blue but, instead, an endless succession of gray, green, and white water that is churning, crashing, and shooting spray into the air.

The plane's radar can do 270-degree sweeps of the water and should be able to pick out a boat and maybe a raft on the ocean. It also has the potential to pick out a person in the water, but not in these conditions. Ahlstrand hopes the EPIRB came from a boat, knowing how difficult it would be for the radar or the human eye to locate a life raft, and near impossible to find a person. Marcus Jones, the navigator, is thinking the same thing. They have already been flying racetrack-pattern loops over the last known position of the EPIRB hit and extending that in the direction of the drift rate, as indicated by the computer models from SAR headquarters. *If anyone is in a raft or the water, being tumbled by those waves,* thinks Jones, *they are probably already dead.*

Suddenly, Jones sits up straight, eyes wide. He thought he heard a faint tone from an electronic signal. He sits motionless, straining to listen through his headset. He hears it again. "Just heard a faint signal!" he shouts. "Probably an EPIRB. Let's go back!" At the same instant he notices a tiny blip on the radar. Then it disappears. He prays it is not just debris.

"MARK, MARK, MARK!"

The plane is moving between 150 to 170 knots per hour, approximately two and a half to three miles per minute. It will be tough to see anything with the naked eye, and Jones is hoping the radar will pick up something on the next pass. The pilots bank the plane, turning in a wide arc back toward the EPIRB hit, flying at just four hundred feet above the ocean. As the C-130 zooms past the location of the signal, Jones is focused on the radar, and the other six crew members are searching the ocean for anything other than water. But neither the radar nor the crew locates any objects in the tempest below. Jones shakes his head. *We are in the right area, but maybe it's just a piece of a boat.*

Rudy and Ben see the plane at the same time. They are down in a trough, looking up at a patch of sky framed on either side by moving walls of green water when, for a brief moment, the plane speeds into view, the orange stripe on its side clearly visible. The wind and waves are so loud, they can barely hear the roar of its engines. The plane is about three hundred yards off to the left and seems to fly a few feet above the seas. Just as quickly, the aircraft is out of sight, blocked by the nearest wave. Both men are too stunned and surprised to say a word, and are barely able to hold back their tears of joy. They think the Coast Guard crew in the plane got a good look at them because they were so close.

JP is conscious and surprises his friends by croaking, "They know we are here . . ." He, too, saw the plane for an instant before it streaked behind the towering waves.

"Yes!" shouts Rudy. "They found us!"

Minutes go by that feel like an eternity. Then the plane appears again. It is still off to the left. Rudy begins to worry. *Maybe they didn't see us. They must have got our original emergency signal but maybe don't know exactly where we are.*

Quickly, he yanks one of the flares he had stuck in the pocket of his raincoat right before exiting the boat. The protective cover must be pulled off and then used to strike the head of the flare to ignite it, similar to lighting a match. The ten-inch handheld flare, once lit, will shoot out a bright flame. Try as he might, Rudy cannot get the flare to light. He curses, tosses it into the ocean, and desperately pulls another one from his pocket. "Damn," he mutters as he strikes it with the cap. He uses all his strength, again and again striking the flare, but nothing will make it light. Shaking with frustration and anger, he hurls this one into the ocean as well, fearing that the C-130 has left for good.

"Have you got any more?" Ben shouts. A particularly large wave bears down on the tiny vessel. Luckily, its sheer wall does not collapse, and it slides beneath the raft.

Rudy digs deep into his pocket and pulls out the last flare. This one is a rocket flare, larger than the others. Rudy is trying to calm himself, but he's got no time to lose. He aims the flare's cylinder-shaped tube directly above the raft and, holding his breath, pulls the string that acts as the trigger.

The flare hisses and then fires upward, a bright orange ball of flame heading toward the gray sky. It is designed to go several hundred feet into the air, but it travels about fifty feet, then is caught by the wind and blown sideways into a wave. *Oh, shit,* thinks Rudy, *the plane can't have seen it.*

"Mark! Mark! Mark!" shouts Marcus Jones. He had moved away from the radar screen to a window and, out of the corner of his eye, for a fraction of a second, spots a glowing streak of orange. He wants the crew to mark the aircraft's position so they can circle back to the exact spot where he saw the light.

Beavis and Ahlstrand put the plane into a steep bank and complete the semicircle bringing them back to the mark. All seven crew members stare out the windows, expecting to see a boat just ahead. But at 150 miles per hour, they get only a quick glimpse of the area, and no one sees a thing except slashing rain pelting the windows and acres of towering white peaks and dark gray valleys below.

Jones waits at the window as the pilots bank the plane once again. He knows what he saw, and it was most definitely a flare. *Where did the boat disappear to? Could it have sunk in just the few minutes since I saw the streak of light? Could it have drifted well beyond the initial mark?*

Beavis speaks through the headsets. "Okay, we are almost back at the marked spot." Jones is at the window, looking a short distance ahead of the plane. He sees something that makes him gasp. A tiny black object, which appears to be the size of a dime, is halfway up the face of a wind-streaked wave. "A raft!" he shouts. "Two o'clock on our right! I think at least one person is on it!"

Some of the others in the plane see it as well, and then, just like that, it's gone from sight. Jones thinks, *That raft didn't even seem inflated. How in the world could anyone stay on it? It was tiny. Maybe it wasn't even a raft but debris from the boat, and one or more persons is hanging on to it.*

Now the rest of the crew gets busy. In the cargo area is something called a MA-3 kit. It is made up of five canvas bags, each about the size of a small trash barrel. In three of the bags are life rafts that will start to inflate as soon as they leave the aircraft. In the remaining two bags are survival supplies such as food, water, whistles, reflecting mirrors, and sunscreen. The bags are stretched out along fifteen hundred feet of line, so there is a better chance that part of the line will be near the survivors. Normally, this is what would be dropped out the rear cargo door, but Commander Beavis is having second thoughts. With hurricane-force winds, he's not sure how far off course the kit will be blown before reaching the water. He decides it's best to drop one raft and see what happens. He also worries that if the survivors leave their partially inflated raft to try and swim to another that is over twenty to thirty feet away, they will drown before they reach it. Through his headset, Beavis tells Casey Green and Ryan Cantu to get ready with a single raft, adding, "In seas this big, the survivors might be better off staying with their own raft unless we can put one right next to them. After you drop our raft, let me know how far from the survivors it lands. We may want to save our other rafts until the survivors' raft starts sinking further or is torn apart."

The drop master acknowledges the instructions and begins to position a single raft at the rear of the plane. It's not an easy job. The back of the aircraft takes the full brunt of the extreme turbulence, shuddering as if the hand of a giant is shaking it. The drop master fights back motion sickness, then opens the cargo door and waits for the plane to circle back toward the survivors. He uses this time to consider when to push the raft out. He knows the survivors' raft—if what they are on is in fact a raft—may be partially inflated, and he figures his raft will drift faster than the survivors' once it hits the ocean. For that reason, he wants his raft to hit the water upwind and forward of the survivors so that it will drift back to them.

The other scanners in the plane tell the drop master they are almost above the survivors. The drop master, peering out the cargo door, soon sees the survivors below and aft of the aircraft and quickly launches his raft. The raft is immediately taken by the wind and seems to be blown horizontally, pushed well to the right of the survivors. With all the foam on the surface of the ocean, it's hard to see exactly where it lands, but the drop master knows it never got near the survivors. He describes what happened to Beavis.

"Okay," says Beavis, "let's hold off on dropping any more equipment. I'm afraid they might try to leave their raft and we'll lose them. It's not just the wind; the survivors' raft is drifting between six and nine knots."

Beavis and Ahlstrand bank the plane once again and return to the spot where the survivors were seen. The raft is gone! Not one of the seven crew members can see it. Ahlstrand is thinking, *We can't lose sight of them now. If we can't find them on our next pass, we may have lost them for good.*

Again they make the loop back to the location, factoring in the raft's quick drift rate, and this time half the crew sees the black raft below. Ahlstrand lets out a sigh of relief. He knows the waves must have blocked the survivors from view and realizes what a challenge it will be not to lose them in the chaos below.

Beavis is on the radio to SAR Headquarters. "We have spotted a life raft or a makeshift life raft with survivors. Not sure how many, but we think we saw two people. We have dropped a raft, but it was blown away. We will attempt to keep the survivors in sight for the Jayhawk. Tell the helo crew that visibility is fair to poor, wind gusts just above eighty knots, and the waves look enormous. We have enough fuel to stay on-scene for another five hours." Commander Beavis gives their location, then signs off. He and his crew have shifted out of the search mode and are going to do their best not to lose visual sight of the target. The pilot and copilot alternate time at the aircraft's controls to ward off fatigue brought on by the extreme flying conditions. It is impossible to keep the plane in any type of steady flight; the altitude indicators are in a constant state of flux, rocking and vacillating wildly. The pilots decide to deploy two flares the next time they pass the raft to help mark its location. These flares, which are water-activated, emit a solid trail of white smoke that on most days can be seen at a great distance and help aircrews visually relocate targets in the water. On this day, the flares and their smoke trails simply vanish, absorbed by the white froth covering the ocean. Beavis knows if they can't keep a visual on the raft when they pass overhead, the men in the water will die.

At SAR Headquarters, Supervisor Geoff Pagels communicates with Beavis. He now knows they have a real emergency with people in a raft associated with the first EPIRB activated, the one registered to a vessel named *Lou Pantai* (actually, the *Sean Seamour II*). The C-130 will stay on-scene, which means he needs to call Elizabeth City and have them assemble a crew for another C-130 to investigate the EPIRB signal from the *Flying Colours*. Pagels has recently gotten a good location fix for that EPIRB from a passing satellite. He is aware that a third vessel, the *Illusion,* has made radio contact with the Coast Guard and is getting pummeled by the seas but is not in an emergency situation.

The contact for the men in the raft is Betty de Lutz, and Pagels has promised her that he will call as soon as he has new information. When he gets Betty on the phone, he says, "Our search plane has located a life raft. We now have to wait for our helicopter to get on-scene for the rescue. The crew of our aircraft tell me there are perhaps two survivors on board."

"No!" Betty shouts "There were three people on the boat!"

"Okay," says Pagels, "I understand. I'll be sure to tell the pilots to look for three people. I will call you back as soon as I have more news."

Pagels alerts both the helo and the C-130 pilots that there should be three people on the raft. Then he takes a deep breath and tries to relax. He knows the flight-ready crew and aircraft from Elizabeth City are stretched thin, so he decides to alert distant air stations such as Cape Cod and keep them apprised of the situation. He is also monitoring the progress of the helicopter that just lifted the family off the *Seeker*, anxious for it to land so he has at least one group of survivors safely accounted for. The juggling act that Pagels is performing reminds him of the nightmare while he was assigned to the cutter *Dallas,* when the space shuttle *Challenger* went down. He hopes the outcome will be different.

Now Pagels gets back on the phone, still trying to make connection with the listed numbers for the EPIRB of the *Flying Colours* to confirm that the vessel is out at sea. While punching in phone numbers, he wonders, *What kind of storm is this that so many vessels are in trouble?*

CHAPTER TWENTY

LIKE A HOCKEY PUCK ON ICE

The excitement of seeing the C-130 does not last long for Ben. About every five or ten minutes, it zips briefly into view between the passing waves. None of the survivors is even aware that the plane dropped a life raft. JP has slipped back into unconsciousness, but Ben and Rudy have talked a little. Both have come to the conclusion that the winds are too much for a helicopter to fly in, and that the C-130 is just trying to keep track of their position until they have to return to land for fuel. Ben thinks that by the time the storm abates enough for a helicopter to launch, he will long since be dead. The raft has been flipped by the waves a total of three times, and each time the process to get back on board has been slower as the men's energy diminishes. Ben sees that JP's lips are purple, and he appears to be unconscious again. If hypothermia doesn't kill JP soon, Ben worries that another capsizing of the raft will drown JP before he and Rudy are able to retrieve him.

The plane sweeps by yet again, and Ben thinks, *This is torture. There is nothing they can do.* He almost wishes the plane never even found them; it just got his hopes up, only to send them plunging back down. But he thinks of his family. *At least now they will know what happened to me, and it might be a bit easier on them.*

Rudy doesn't even look at the plane when it passes by. It hurts too much to lift his head and expose his skin to the stinging rain. He's beginning to feel angry that the plane has circled the raft for so long. *They are keeping a death watch. Why don't they just go away and end this vigil . . .*

Time drags on. For the next two hours, the plane circles while the men below do their best to stay with the raft. It seems the raft is

133

riding lower in the water and might have a leak, but it's impossible to know for sure or to find the source of any escaping air. It barely matters if the raft is right side up or upside down; in both positions, it is like sitting in the middle of a trampoline filled with water.

JP drifts in and out of consciousness, occasionally moaning when a wave rattles his broken ribs especially hard. In his lucid moments, he is aware that the Coast Guard knows their location. He is also cognizant of the fact that a helicopter won't fly in such wind and that even a large Coast Guard cutter or ship couldn't make any real headway in such seas and certainly couldn't do a rescue. He thinks it's a miracle that the C-130 found them so far from land, and he hopes that Ben and Rudy can somehow last another day. Then he feels himself sinking back toward oblivion, welcoming its embrace.

C-130 Aircraft Commander Beavis gives Jayhawk helicopter pilot Nevada Smith the coordinates and drift rate of the raft. Both Nevada and his copilot, Aaron Nelson, are elated: They won't have to waste precious fuel and time searching. Nevada plugs the coordinates into the aircraft navigation system and establishes a point where they can intercept the raft. Aaron starts thinking about the return trip or where they might need to go to refuel. Marine Corps Air Station Cherry Point, North Carolina, located 110 miles south of Elizabeth City, looks like a good choice because the winds will be with them. Aaron estimates that they will have close to one hour to perform the rescue. *We have time,* Aaron thinks, *and that means everything, with conditions this bad.*

Flight Mechanic Scott Higgins and Rescue Swimmer Drew Dazzo have been listening to the radio exchange between the C-130 and their helo. Scott turns to Drew and says, "Well, we're really going to do a rescue. No false alarm here."

When the helicopter pilots are near where they expect the raft to be, they descend to three hundred feet. They hold in a hover, scanning the seas. All they can see is wave after towering wave. Wind blasts rock the helicopter every which way, putting the pilot on edge. Nevada is so awestruck by the maelstrom below that he picks up his video camera and films the scene.

Scott opens up the aircraft doorway, and the wailing wind whips through the cabin with a strange sucking sound. Drew and Scott are on their bellies, and they slide to the open door and poke their heads out, a sensation similar to sticking your head out the sunroof of a racecar going 150 miles per hour. The view is like looking down on the Swiss Alps—snowcapped summits and dark valleys. But these mountains are moving, all advancing in the same direction. The sight makes the two men a bit dizzy, but they scour the waves below for sight of a raft. An occasionally strong gust causes the aircraft to shudder as if they are in a paint mixer, and the men tighten their grip on the doorframe.

Over the radio, Nevada contacts Beavis, saying, "We still can't see them."

Beavis, circling the C-130 above the Jayhawk, answers, "Follow me. We're about to go right over them."

Scott, hanging his head out the doorway, instinctively flinches as he sees the C-130 pass close by.

The C-130 roars a couple hundred feet past the HH-60 Jayhawk. Rain splatters on the helo's windshield in such volume that the wipers have a hard time keeping up. Nevada watches the C-130 bank hard.

"Hey, Nevada," says Beavis, "they're off our wing right now."

Nevada and the crew look into the white and gray mess below. "Still don't see them," says Nevada.

"Turn to two o'clock. Do you see them now?" asks Beavis.

"No."

"You're almost directly over them. Look forward just a bit and off to your right."

Nevada looks at an oncoming wave. About halfway up the wave is a small black object. *Holy shit,* thinks Nevada, *these waves are even bigger than I thought. They must be seventy feet!* The eight-foot life raft is the first thing to contrast with the waves, and it looks minuscule compared to the towering seas. Imagine the wave is the size of an eight-by-ten sheet of paper. Now imagine the raft is the size of a small button, no more than a quarter inch across. That is what Nevada is seeing, and it makes him gasp, especially when the top part of the wave—fifteen feet of churning white water—bears down on the raft. Nevada is afraid that when it reaches the vessel, it will engulf it completely and there will be no one alive to rescue. But somehow the raft floats over the foam, teeters on the mountaintop, and then slides wildly down the back side of the wave into the valley below.

Scott and Drew, squinting into the windblown rain, see the raft a second or two after the pilots, and their initial impression is the same as Nevada's: The waves are unlike anything they have ever seen. Scott thinks, *Oh my God. These waves are triple the size I guessed earlier. The raft is just flying along, it's doing over six knots. This won't be easy.* Drew—the one who has to go down into those waves—feels a surge of adrenaline, as if someone took a needle and mainlined it into his veins. *How in the hell are we ever going to do this? Those people on the raft are getting the crap kicked out of them.* It's not just the size of the waves that has Drew's heart racing, but also their steepness and the churning foam everywhere. He sees a wave break, and he tries to imagine being slammed under by the avalanching water. *If I get buried by one of those, it's going to push me down like a pile driver.* He begins to consider how long it will take to claw back to the surface, then shakes his head. *Do not think about it. Stay positive. You can do this.*

Nevada is back on the radio to Beavis. "Okay, we see it, looks like there are two or maybe three people on the raft." To Aaron, sitting next to him, he says, "Can you believe this?"

"It's unreal," Aaron answers.

"I've never seen waves like this, not even close. The raft looks like a hockey puck on ice, the way it's moving."

Beavis breaks in. "Okay, we will be circling above you at sixteen hundred feet." The commander of the C-130 climbs to sixteen hundred feet, where the plane will be better able to conserve fuel and stay at a safe distance from the Jayhawk. At that altitude, the plane is in or above the clouds and will have no visual contact with either the helicopter or the raft. Beavis will monitor what is happening below via radio, and if Nevada loses sight of the raft, the rescue swimmer, or a survivor in the water, he can swoop down and assist in the search.

Aaron, who is doing most of the flying, lowers the helicopter to 120 feet above the cavernous wave troughs. The circulating air from the rotor wash makes the water below them look like a blizzard. Aaron has the helo's nose into the wind, which uses the least amount of power in a hover. For the first time, he is thankful for the wind—he can use less torque on the hover, which leaves a bigger power margin should one engine fail. He manages power by a lever to his left, a collective, and he controls direction via a lever directly in front of him and extending up between his legs, a cyclic.

Nevada cons Aaron to a position directly behind the raft, and they hold there to allow Scott and Drew to get ready for the deployment. At this low altitude, the crew has a much better view of the half-submerged black raft, and they can see that there are three people hanging on to it. Every now and then a blast of wind hits the helo so hard, the crew loses sight of the raft. Sometimes the raft is out of sight simply because of the size of the waves. Nevada thinks about each man's job and how difficult it will be. *No matter what,* he tells himself, *once Drew goes in the water, we need to keep him in sight.*

Nevada alerts Beavis on the C-130, saying, "We've got a good look at the raft, and there are three people. Two are wearing yellow gear, but one [Ben] is in dark red and hard to pick out from the raft. That's why you couldn't see him. Our flight mech and swimmer are getting ready, and we will try to do a basket hoist." He turns to Aaron. "Can we get a little lower?"

"Roger."

The copilot lowers the helicopter another twenty feet.

Despite the swirling foam and spray, Drew can see the wave tops clearly. He thinks he can save time by going into the water without the cable if he times his jump into the highest point of the wave. Through his headset, he says to Nevada, "Can we do a free-fall deployment?"

"Do you really think that's the safest way to enter the water?" asks Nevada, trying to tamp down Drew's adrenaline.

Drew rethinks his approach. "You're right. I'll go down on the strop."

Nevada knows rescue swimmers live for this kind of moment, and that Drew would jump into a volcano if that were needed. He also knows the risk. The rescue swimmer can lose his mask or a fin, or a survivor can choke him. And the swimmer will most definitely be ingesting seawater and working in a state of near exhaustion. In fact, Nevada considers the rescue swimmer another PIW (person in water) who could be in an emergency situation of his own. The commander takes that a step further and considers that the operation will have a total of six rescues/hoists: the three people on the raft plus three times hoisting Drew. (The rescue swimmer will need to be retrieved after getting each survivor in the basket, because the raft will have blown far away, and the swimmer will need to be brought back up and then repositioned for the next drop. The basket is too small to bring up both Drew and a survivor at the same time.)

Suddenly, Aaron says, "Did you see that?"

"What?" says Nevada.

"The radar altimeter just went from a hundred to twenty."

"Incredible."

"That's an eighty-foot wave!"

"I'll start calling out the big waves."

Aaron knows Scott will need the helo as low as possible to hoist the survivors, but the copilot has made up his mind that his top objective will be to provide a margin of safety between the aircraft and any rogue waves. *Just listen to Nevada, do what Scott says, and keep an eye on the second wave crest coming at us.* There is so much going on that Aaron needs to keep it simple. *Stay relaxed, we have time. Take it slow. If it takes more than one attempt to get the first man, that's okay.*

Aaron has his priorities, and number one is to avoid having a wave sneak up on him and clip the underside of the helo. With waves this big, that's a real possibility, and if that happens, it's all over for both survivors and aircrew.

CHAPTER TWENTY-ONE

DEPLOYING THE SWIMMER

JP's stepmother, Betty de Lutz, is pacing the floor of her Cape Cod home. She has been up half the night, ever since the first call from the Coast Guard. Now she has just received a call from the Coast Guard saying they have spotted a life raft.

Betty has a difficult decision to make. Should she call JP's wife, Mayke, to let her know that the *Sean Seamour II* sank in a storm and a Coast Guard plane has spotted a raft? Mayke surely deserves to know what is happening, but Betty hesitates because of the reference the Coast Guard contact made in the last conversation to two people in the raft rather than three. That sent a chill up Betty's spine and prompted her to pray harder. *What if one of the men is dead and swept away? It could be JP . . . I won't call Mayke until I know for certain if JP is dead or alive. And if he's alive, I won't call until I can tell her if he is okay or injured.*

Betty is startled out of her ruminations by the telephone. Instead of picking it up on the first ring, she says a quick prayer. "Please God, let them find all three men." Then she answers the phone.

"Mrs. de Lutz, this is Geoff Pagels from the Coast Guard."

"Yes. Tell me what is happening."

"We now have a helicopter at the emergency scene, in addition to an orbiting C-130 plane. The helicopter pilots were able to get low enough to see clearly into the life raft."

Betty doesn't breathe. The next sentence means everything.

"The pilots tell us there are three people in the raft. They are just about to lower the rescue swimmer. Once they do that, they will begin hoisting the survivors up."

"So they are alive?"

"We think so. At least one is alive, because a flare was fired from the raft, so chances are the others are alive as well. But this is a bad storm. These are experienced pilots, and they have never seen waves like the ones on-scene."

"What else can you tell me?"

"That's all we know. But as soon as I learn more, I'll call you."

"Thank you. Thank you so much," says Betty, her voice trailing off. She sits heavily in a chair, drained of energy but relieved. *I'm not going to call Mayke until that man calls me back and says JP is alive and well and in the helicopter.*

Betty has no idea that across the ocean on a hilltop in France, Mayke is in her studio, staring into space, unable to paint, because she has an unshakable feeling that something awful has happened to JP.

JP, slumped in Rudy's arms, is unconscious, totally unaware of the image appearing above him. From seemingly out of nowhere, a helicopter is hovering directly overhead, its rotor wash sending out circular bands of spray snatched up from the ocean, pelting the survivors. Rudy is so startled that he thinks maybe he's hallucinating. The helicopter is just a hundred feet overhead. He can see the orange Coast Guard stripe and the open cabin door.

Ben, too, is caught off guard. The waves surrounding them are so tall that he could not see the helicopter approach and could not hear its engine above the blasting wind. Now the sight of this giant steel aircraft so near their little raft is more than he can process. It's a surreal experience, as if he's watching a movie about someone else's life and rescue. But the helicopter stays in place, and Ben knows it's real. He feels euphoric. Just a minute earlier he had no hope and was waiting for the inevitable conclusion. Now salvation has come down out of the clouds. He also wonders how in the world the rescuers will get them off the raft with three-story waves crashing and colliding all around.

Rescue swimmer Drew Dazzo checks his dry suit one last time, making sure the seals are tight while telling the others he is going off the internal communication system. He removes his headset and puts on his fins, mask and snorkel, gloves, and finally, his neon-yellow

140

rescue helmet. Then he puts on the gunner's belt that extends to a secure point on the wall opposite the cabin door, and he waits for the flight mechanic, Scott Higgins, to get in position. The gunner's belt will be removed just before he is lowered.

He and Scott have talked about the rescue steps, and because the raft is moving so fast, Scott has told Drew not to even try to get back to the raft after the first survivor is in the basket. Instead, Scott will lower the strop, and they can either ferry Drew to the raft without him returning to the helicopter or, if the raft has moved a great distance, bring Drew back up and redeploy when the pilots relocate the raft.

Scott motions for Drew to come to the door, and the rescue swimmer moves into a sitting position at the edge of the doorframe. Scott hands him the hook and strop, and Drew secures the nylon sling under his arms. While all this is going on, Scott is letting the pilots know exactly what is happening, painting a verbal picture of the action, using scripted language. It's imperative that everything Scott says through his headset is clear and precise. He will also do the conning—instructions to the pilots for positioning the aircraft so the swimmer can be lowered as close as possible to the raft.

"The door is open," says Scott to Nevada and Aaron. "The swimmer is at the door and ready."

Scott is wearing leather gloves so he won't cut his hands on the cable. In his right hand is a pendant attached to a long wire cord that controls the hoist, which is suspended from a steel arm extending from the airframe above the door. Scott also has on a gunner's belt and safety strap: He will be spending a fair amount of time leaning out of the aircraft, and should he slip, the gunner's belt and strap will keep him from tumbling into the sea. He is in a kneeling position and cranes his head out of the doorway to get a better look at the raft and waves. The wind literally snatches the breath right out of him. In all his prior rescues, the wind never exceeded thirty knots, and now he's being blasted by eighty-to-eighty-five-knot gusts. It's impossible to talk, and he's winded within a minute, but he does get a good look at the waves and notices that every third one is a bit bigger than the two before it. He's trying to get a feel for the seas and wants to be sure that he times Drew's descent so the swimmer isn't going into one of the larger waves.

Nevada gives the go-ahead for deployment.

Scott taps Drew on the chest, the signal that he is ready. Drew removes the gunner's belt, then gives his partner the thumbs-up sign that he, too, is ready to be lowered and begin the rescue.

"Deploying the swimmer."

Using the pendant, Scott pulls up a bit of cable while Drew leans out the doorway until he is in the air. Scott keeps a hand on Drew to keep him from being blown back into the airframe, and then he slowly releases cable and Drew starts his descent.

"Swimmer is outside the cabin. Swimmer is being lowered."

Drew is amazed by the power of the wind pushing him back toward the rear of the aircraft. A strap from his mask is hitting his helmet, making a loud "clack, clack, clack" sound in rapid fire. His fins are acting like kites, catching the wind and pulling him aft. Drew's head is on a swivel, trying to locate the raft below while being blown and spun by the wind. He is streaming far aft of the helicopter, so that the raft is much too far away, way out in front of him.

Drew, dangling at the end of the cable, is absolutely blown away by the size of the waves. *This is going to be interesting.* He's glad he elected to go down by strop, because if he were on the hook, he would have to be lowered into the water, and a wave might drop out from under him before he has a chance to unhook. That would mean he'd fall to the end of the cable slack, when he'd be jerked to a stop like a rag doll. With the strop, he has more control, because all he has to do is raise his arms and he's free.

Up in the helicopter cabin, Scott is on his stomach, using all his strength to push the cable forward, to keep it away from the tail rotor, the external fuel tank, and the back end of the sliding cabin door. He's using every bit of muscle in his six-foot frame, and his voice is strained as he conns the pilots to move the aircraft forward. The helo lurches ahead, and now the rescue swimmer is a bit too forward of the raft. "Back twenty feet," says Scott. Aaron eases up on the power, but the winds are so strong that the Jayhawk shoots farther back. Scott shouts, "Hold, hold, hold!"

The sheer force of the wind has taken all fluidity out of the helicopter's movements, and it flies erratically. To Scott, it seems the helo's motions are at warp speed, and instead of calmly saying, "Back right forty, back right thirty, back right twenty," he's barking out positions in staccato style.

"Okay, forward ten feet." The helicopter lumbers forward into the wind, but the raft is drifting so fast that they have overshot it. Scott has done many hoists off moving boats, but the raft's movements are hard to time. When it is in the trough of a wave, it slows down, but when the next wave reaches it, the raft shoots forward with the wave, increasing speed as it climbs the wave, where the power of the wind also propels it forward.

"Ease back ten feet. Good, now hold! Swimmer is in position!"

Drew is within about ten feet of the wave crests but a full eighty feet from the troughs. The raft, sliding with the seas, is about thirty feet away, and he realizes Scott has gotten him as close as he can. Drew knows it's time, knows he's got to do this just right. He feels an electric jolt of energy course through his body as he watches a big roller rumble toward him. When the snarling crest passes five feet below, Drew raises his arms and plunges out of the strop.

Scott's eyes widen as he watches Drew hit the water while the cable and the strop go whipping toward the rear of the aircraft. "Damn!" he mutters. He's retracting the cable as fast as possible, worried it will get jammed in the external fuel tank. Even when he has the hook and strop in hand, he's concerned. *It's going to be near impossible to get either the basket or the hook back to Drew. How the hell do I explain to his wife I couldn't get him back.*

Aaron has let the helicopter slide back so that he and Nevada can get a visual on Drew. Nevada is craning forward. "I can see Drew," he says. Aaron risks a brief look down and to his right, but mostly, he is sitting almost stone-still, lightly working the cyclic and collective, focused 100 percent on keeping the Jayhawk at an even altitude and following the conning from either Nevada or Scott.

"Big wave coming," says Nevada in as calm a voice as possible.

Aaron was watching the same approaching wave, and he powers up another ten feet. The wave is a monster and rolls past, and Aaron thinks, *If we hadn't spotted that one coming, that could have been way too close.*

CHAPTER TWENTY-TWO

"HE NEEDS TO GO FIRST . . ."

The second Drew hit the water, he started swimming as fast as he could. Now he's trying to go even faster, afraid that he won't catch the raft before a wave breaks and buries him in its churning fury. If that happens, he'll have to start all over again by being ferried to the raft or hoisted back to the helicopter and then repositioned. Foam is coming through his snorkel, so he's barely taking a breath. He's got to get to the raft, and is already wondering if he can do this three times.

Rudy and Ben are amazed that the rescue swimmer is in the water and actually gaining on the raft. The tension they feel, being this close to rescue, is unbelievable. Then a wave slides between the raft and the swimmer, blocking their view, and they wonder if he's still making progress. When the wave rolls by, the swimmer is at the side of the raft.

Drew puts an elbow on the raft, spits out his snorkel, takes two deep breaths, then looks at the men and says, "How y'all doing today?"

Ben is so flabbergasted by what he has just seen and heard that all he can do is smile. Rudy simply says, "You guys are fucking amazing!"

Drew is relieved to hear that comment. When he first looked at Rudy's eyes, they seemed as wide as garbage can lids, and Drew was afraid the survivor was about to panic. Now he knows the man with the gray beard is not just lucid but has kept his sense of humor. Drew nods and says, "Thank you. Is anyone hurt?"

The rescue swimmer is processing information as quickly as he can, first noting that the raft is in bad shape, that the men do not have survival suits on, and one of the men seems unresponsive.

Ben and Rudy point down at JP. Rudy says, "He is. Broken ribs. He needs to go first."

"All right, he's coming with me first."

Drew sizes up JP. He looks half dead, barely hanging on.

Scott is pulling the basket bails together so he can insert the hook through their tops. The basket is a metal cage about two and a half feet wide by four feet long, and on each end are floats so that the top of the basket will ride even with the ocean's surface. Survivors sit with their knees bent and involuntarily hold on to its sides with a viselike grip. Although it is designed to hold six hundred pounds, there is not enough room in it to hoist two people. In some rescues, the strop is used so that the rescue swimmer and the victim can be hoisted together, but that carries more risk for the survivor, who might slip out of the strop. And it is not an option for JP, who is unable to help in the rescue.

Working inside the cabin, Scott is facing away from the doorway. This is the first time he cannot see Drew, and he's concerned, racing to complete the task. As soon as the basket is on the hook, Scott moves back to the doorway, lies on his stomach, and waits for Drew to let him know when he is ready with the first survivor. He feels like he is watching a science fiction movie play out below. Few people on earth have ever seen waves this big, and it's almost inconceivable that men are in the middle of it and still alive. He can see Drew's neon-yellow helmet at the side of the raft, and he knows Drew will be hollering out the procedure for rescue to the survivors.

Come on, come on, frets Scott, *hurry up.* He's anxious to start lowering the metal cage, knowing that it might take several attempts to reposition the helo and get the basket close enough for Drew and the first survivor to reach it. Scott also wonders about the first survivor to be taken from the raft. *Jeez, I hope he's cooperative. Drew's never going to pull this off with a panicked and aggressive victim.*

In the cockpit, Aaron can feel the beads of sweat trickling down his chest inside his dry suit. Now that the rescue swimmer is in the water and they are waiting to lower the basket, he has climbed in altitude, to be on the safe side. In calmer weather, he could put the helicopter in the automated "altitude hold" function, but with the seas gyrating below, that's not an option; the aircraft would be bolting up and down wildly with each passing wave. For Scott to do his job, he needs the Jayhawk as stable as possible, and the best way to do that is in a manual hover.

Aaron cannot see Drew or the life raft, but one thought has been bothering him for the last few minutes: *This is taking an awful long time.* He's worried the seas are overpowering the rescue swimmer and the wind will be too much for the hoist operator to perform a safe extraction of survivors. He's also reconsidering his earlier thought that they would have plenty of fuel so they could take their time with the rescues. With everything moving much slower than normal, Aaron is concerned that they'll bump up against their bingo time before they can complete the mission. And if they have to leave anyone down in the water or in the damaged raft, that's as good as a death sentence.

As if reading his mind, Nevada says, "Scott should be lowering the basket any second. Do you need a break? Do you want me to fly?"

"I'm okay."

"You're doing great."

A gust rocks the helo. Nevada thinks, *Thank God for our mechanics.* He knows that all the hours of maintenance and repairs put in back at the air station make the difference between success or aborting the mission or even catastrophe. *It's going slow,* Nevada reasons, *but everyone is calm and doing their job.*

"Turn him around!" shouts Drew, referring to JP. "I want his back by the edge of the raft!"

Rudy and Ben slide the unconscious captain around and to the side of the raft. Drew puts his arms under JP's and pulls the survivor's back in tight to his chest. He then uses his feet to push against the raft and drags JP out.

JP stirs, and his eyes flutter open. He's got this awful sensation that someone is choking him, a sensation he is all too familiar with because that's what his father would do to him to make a point. He's too weak and confused to fight back. He feels like he's in the water, but if that's true, how could his father be choking him? A voice in his ear says, "We're going for a basket ride."

Drew has no idea whether JP has heard him or is processing what he's saying. For now the rescue swimmer is relieved that the injured man isn't moving. He has JP in what is called a cross-chest carry, with his right arm over JP's right shoulder and his hand under JP's left armpit. The maneuver allows him to tow JP a short distance from the raft.

Looking up at the helicopter, Drew gives the thumbs-up sign that he is ready for the basket. He knows Scott or the pilots have seen him because the aircraft immediately moves forward while descending. A wave partially breaks on the men, pushing them both under, and Drew does his best to raise JP's head above the foam.

Scott slides the basket to the doorway. With his left hand, he pushes it outside the cabin while, with his right hand, he works the pendant, and the basket begins its descent. The wind blows it toward the back of the aircraft. Scott, who is now on his stomach, wrestles with the cable, pulling it forward so that the basket and cable don't get pushed into the tail rotor or the external fuel tank.

Nevada is scanning the instruments and alerting the C-130 of their progress while keeping his eye on the clock and the oncoming waves. He's growing fretful about the slow pace due to the seas. As quietly and calmly as possible, he says, "How's it going back there, Scott?"

"Basket is being lowered," gasps Scott.

From Drew's perspective, the deployment is not going well. The basket is streaming about thirty feet behind the aircraft on about 130 feet of cable. Drew snatches a glimpse of Scott in the doorway, struggling with the cable. The Jayhawk slowly advances past his position in the ocean, bringing the trailing basket closer. Drew is having a hard time seeing the basket because of the foam scudding along the ocean's surface like tumbleweed rolling through a desert. The downdrafts from the helicopter's rotors add to the chaos, sending a swirling froth in all directions. Drew surges upward, using his flippers to gain a bit of height, and sees that the basket is only twenty-five feet away. He makes his move, knifing through the water with JP under one arm. Just a few feet before his objective, out of the corner of his eye, he sees a wave looming overhead. He grabs a bite of air before he and JP are pummeled by collapsing white water of such force that Drew is stunned and truly frightened. *Whatever happens, don't let go of this man,* Drew tells himself. He's not sure which way is up or down, but he tries to stay calm, knowing that the buoyancy in his dry suit, coupled with JP's PFD, will bring them to the surface. When his head clears the foam, he has swallowed a good deal of seawater, and he wonders if the limp man in his arms is still alive. Drew treads water and steals a look at JP, noting his quivering purple lips, yet he's surprised to see the survivor's eyes open.

The basket is now far away, and Drew waits, knowing Scott will vector the pilots back into position, where the cage will be closer. He watches the aircraft maneuvering for another pass, determined not to miss the opportunity. When the basket is ten feet away, Drew rushes forward to grab it. This time he almost has a hand on its metal bars when the wave beneath him drops away, and rescue swimmer and survivor go sliding down its back side while the basket is airborne with no water beneath it.

Drew can't believe it. He's wasting valuable energy, and he doesn't even have the first survivor in the basket. He has no idea how much time has gone by since he entered the water, but it seems like a lot. *Ten minutes? Twenty minutes?* And getting the survivor in the basket is sometimes the hardest part, particularly if the survivor can't help in the process or if he resists, a distinct possibility with hypothermic survivors who cannot think clearly.

Up above, Scott is pissed. He's still on his belly, straining against the gunner's belt, holding the cable forward with his left hand while working the hoist with his right. Because the basket is far behind the helicopter, he has to keep his eyes on that spot rather than looking ahead for oncoming waves. He is conning the pilots into a position thirty feet in front of the men in the water below, but he is also listening for Nevada to warn him of any really big waves approaching. *This is taking way too long. Wonder what the fuel situation is.* Then he stops the thought sharply. *That's the pilots' concern. Just focus on your job.*

The aircraft crew members aren't the only ones anxious about the passing time. Rudy and Ben, still in the drifting raft, are now far from the action. They can no longer see JP and the rescue swimmer, and with each passing wave, their glimpses of the helicopter are becoming briefer and briefer, until it's mostly out of sight.

Rudy is cold to the core, and he's having trouble gripping the raft's lifeline. *Something's wrong,* he thinks, *but they won't leave us. You made it this far, you can hang tough a little longer.*

CHAPTER TWENTY-THREE

AS IF SHOT FROM A CANNON

Once again Scott has conned the pilots into position and manipulated the cable so that the basket is just ten feet from Drew and JP. Drew makes his move, dragging the survivor with a burst of renewed energy, knowing he has to get JP into the basket before they are carried to a wave crest. This time his free hand grabs hold of one of the metal bars surrounding the cage. He feels the seconds ticking by: The worst scenario would be if only half of JP's body is in the basket when a wave drops out from under them. The slack in the cable will instantly snap taut, and without water to support the basket, any number of injuries can befall JP, including getting his neck broken by the abrupt motion.

Drew pivots to pull JP up to the side bar of the basket and, continuing that motion, gets the semiconscious survivor's torso inside. He feels a wave lifting them up. The rescue swimmer puts one arm under JP's legs and heaves upward with all his might. He's got two thirds of JP inside the basket, and he quickly picks up the survivor's dangling legs and jams them inside as well. Not wasting a moment, he holds on to the side bar with one hand and begins to use the other to give the thumbs-up signal to Scott. But as he's doing so, a jagged wave crest passes beneath them. The basket is ripped from Drew's grip, and he looks up to see JP and the basket go shooting skyward as if ejected from a cannon.

Up above, Scott sees the whole episode play out, holding his breath as the basket jerks violently at the end of the cable. *Damn,* he curses to himself, *we're killing the survivor before we even rescue him.*

The burly flight mechanic is on his knees at the open doorway, retracting the cable as fast as it will go to pull the survivor up. When

150

the basket is at the door, Scott leans out and uses each of his hands to grab different bails. JP's back is to Scott, and he is slumped in an awkward reclining position, with his knees fully bent. It looks like he has been stuffed into the basket and then forcibly jammed down. Scott has no idea whether JP is dead or alive. The survivor's head is underneath a yellow inflatable PFD that has risen and, instead of being around his chest and neck, is wrapped around his face.

For better traction, Scott lifts his left leg so that his foot is on the floor, and then he muscles the steel cage partway into the aircraft, giving JP a real jolt. Then Scott pulls straight back and slides the basket toward the rear of the cabin.

Suddenly, like Lazarus rising from the dead, JP lifts an arm, then struggles to sit up straight. Scott, still kneeling behind JP, grabs him under the arms and starts lifting while JP pushes with his feet, raising his butt from the bottom of the basket. Incredibly, JP arches his back so that it is on the side of the basket, and then he rolls out. The broken ribs take a real pounding, but so many of JP's senses are awakening at once that he barely feels it. His mind is slowly starting to process his surroundings. *I'm not dead. Someone is helping me.*

Scott helps the survivor toward a bench opposite the open doorway, and JP sits. Part of his ashen face is now showing above his PFD, and he looks like a zombie. His expression is dazed, and his eyes stare blankly. The noise from the helicopter is deafening, and it seems to cause JP to come out of shock. He looks around and realizes he is inside a helicopter.

As JP's brain kicks into full consciousness, his first thought is: *Where are the others? They can't be gone, they can't be dead.*

In the cockpit, Aaron feels a bit of relief that one survivor is in the cabin, but now his concern is directed at Drew. Compared to the life raft, Drew is a mere speck in the ocean, a much smaller visual target. Aaron repositions the helo closer to Drew. The rescue swimmer is down in a trough and can barely be seen. *If we lose sight of him, we will never find him.*

Nevada hurriedly shouts, "Large wave approaching!"

Aaron quickly nudges up the power to climb out of danger. He then watches as the colossal roller sweeps up the rescue swimmer and carries him skyward. Drew is lifted so high, he is almost at the same level as Aaron. *Man, I can see his face!* thinks Aaron. The copilot is sitting stock-still; one would never know his pulse is racing. His mind is galloping ahead as well, trying to visualize the next steps. *We're going to be damned lucky if we can get him back . . . and even luckier if we get those remaining on the raft.*

Aaron considers asking Nevada if he thinks they can successfully hoist the swimmer back. He wants reassurance. But he says nothing, telling himself, *Now is not the time.*

Down in the cauldron, Drew is winded. His heart feels like it's going to jump out of his dry suit. After being lifted by the big wave toward the nose of the helo, he's now being pushed aft of the aircraft and directly behind it. Thinking he's in a blind spot, he swims forward and out to the two o'clock position. Another wave pushes him back, this one dunking and spinning him. He surfaces quickly and looks skyward. The helicopter is gone. Just a few seconds ago he felt like he could reach out and grab its landing gear, and now, walled in between two waves, the swimmer can see only a small patch of empty sky overhead. Nor can he hear the rotors amid the wind roaring and waves crashing. Briefly, he thinks the helicopter might have crashed, then he tells himself to stay positive. *You've got the best pilots up there.* Craning his neck, he tries to see more sky and less wave, but no sight of the aircraft. He's not sure which way to swim, so he floats and tries to catch his breath. The enormousness of the waves and the seriousness of his predicament fully dawn on him. *What did I get myself into?*

Scott is back at his perch by the cabin door. He had a brief view of Drew, but now he's nowhere to be seen. "Back fifty feet," he commands through his headset. The flight mechanic lies down on his stomach and shimmies the upper part of his body as far out as he dares, looking beneath the aircraft. "I see the swimmer! Go back ten more feet."

JP is anxiously watching Scott. He isn't sure what's going on, but he knows it's not good. He doesn't have a headset on, so he didn't hear Scott say that he saw Drew. Even though the door is open, the helicopter is warmer than the water, and JP is thinking a bit more clearly. *They can't find the swimmer or the raft.* He can feel panic rising, yet there is not a damn thing he can do.

"Lowering the hook for swimmer," announces Scott. *It would be nice if I could actually see the swimmer longer than a second or two.* Instead of lowering the strop, Scott is lowering the bare hook for less wind resistance.

As the helicopter finally comes into Drew's field of vision, he thinks it's the most beautiful sight he's ever seen. He's so elated, so focused on the hook coming down, that he gets blindsided by a wave breaking directly on him. He's underwater longer than the last time he was buried, and his body is screaming that it needs air. Not sure which way is up, he starts to kick with his flippers, hoping he's heading in the right direction.

About three seconds later, his head clears the surface, and he immediately sucks in a deep breath through his snorkel. He's rewarded with a mouth full of seawater and starts choking. Kicking hard with his flippers, he gets his head above the foam and finally grabs a bite of air. He feels nauseated, spent. Being in a dry suit isn't helping matters—he feels like he's swimming inside it, not from seawater but from his own sweat. The water temperature is 70 degrees, but it could easily have been in the upper 50s if they were just a few miles away, outside the Gulf Stream eddy. If he can't get safely back on the helicopter, the dry suit just might save his life.

Earlier he and Scott decided that once the first survivor was safely aboard, Drew would be "air-taxied" back to the raft instead of being hoisted into the helicopter. This would be quicker than another redeployment. Now Drew is having second thoughts. He's thinking about the way JP shot up into the air on the basket and wonders if the strop is the way to go for the next rescue. *Maybe I should talk to Scott.* He's also thinking that being in the helo for a minute will allow him to breathe real air, not foam and mist. He needs to get his wind back, but he doesn't want to leave the men in the raft any longer than he has to. *I'll decide once I'm airborne.*

In an effort to reduce the gyrations of the cable, the pilots are keeping the helicopter low, just ninety feet above the wave trough. Still, the hook is a moving target. When the hook is ten feet away,

Drew swims to it. Grabbing it is difficult; one minute it is five feet above him and out of reach, and the next it is underwater. He's leery about snatching the cable itself, worried that it might shred his hand if a wave drops out from under him. Finally, in the relative safety of a trough, he grabs hold of the hook.

Drew is wearing a body harness with straps that wrap around the waist, under the legs, up the back, and over the shoulders, then down the chest to reconnect at the waist. He quickly attaches the hook to a point on his waist and gives the thumbs-up sign, relieved to be connected to the aircraft.

Scott announces, "Swimmer is on the hook." He retracts some line so that Drew is just above the wave tops. "Swimmer is one-third up. We can air-taxi him to the raft." Scott has no idea where the raft is but assumes the pilots can either see it or will start searching downwind.

Aaron eases off the power, allowing the wind to push back the helicopter. The wind blows it too hard, making it lurch, and the copilot struggles to stabilize it and slow the speed.

Down below, Drew is skimming just over the wave tops at the end of the hoist line. He makes up his mind that he needs to talk to Scott, and he pats the top of his head, which is the signal to be brought in. Immediately, the cable starts lifting him, though the blasts of wind push Drew in long arcing swings like the pendulum of a clock, making the rescue swimmer dizzy.

Nevada's head is in constant motion. One second he is looking ahead to call out any really large waves, and the next he's watching the cabin door, eager for Drew to appear on the hook. When the swimmer is up and inside, Nevada clenches and pumps his fist with pride. He likens this rescue to a boxing match, with Drew as the fighter who has just gotten through round one. Instead of sitting in his corner of the ring, Drew is sitting on the floor, completely out of breath. He hears Scott say, "Are you okay?" Drew nods and then pukes on the cabin floor.

If Drew is the fighter, Scott is the trainer, and he's watching his man closely, making sure he is a "go" for the next round. "Are you sure you can do this?" he asks.

Catching his breath, Drew says to Scott, "I'll be fine. What do you think about using the strop for the next rescue?"

Scott pauses, thinking how the wave fell out from under the basket just as JP was stuffed in it. "I don't think the strop will be any different. You and the survivor could be jerked even harder on the strop. It would save time, but the more I think about it, the more I think it's too risky."

Drew nods, deferring to Scott, since the flight mechanic will be the one managing the hoist.

Nevada can hear Scott's side of the conversation, knows what they are talking about, and agrees. He turns forward and assists Aaron in searching for the raft. "How you holding up?" he asks.

"Good. But this is unreal. I don't see the raft anywhere."

"Well, it was drifting faster than I've ever seen a raft or a boat drift."

"Let's hope it's still afloat."

CHAPTER TWENTY-FOUR

THEY'RE NOT COMING FOR US

Rudy and Ben clutch the battered raft while wave after wave send it surging forward, away from where they last saw the helicopter. Ten minutes have gone by, and Rudy privately wonders if the pilots decided to return to base before the storm causes a catastrophe. As a pilot himself, he can't blame them.

Ben has been searching the one patch of sky he can see between thundering rollers. He quietly says, "They're not coming for us."

"If they got one, they'll get all three of us." Rudy is nowhere near as confident as his answer indicates. In fact, he's thinking, *We don't even know if the rescue swimmer made it back up to the helo.* No sooner does he complete the thought than the helicopter zips over a wave, about a hundred yards off to the right. "They're still here!" shouts the Canadian.

The helicopter is out of sight for a moment, and then it is back, this time flying to a spot directly above the raft, where it holds in a hover.

"Okay," says Ben, "you go next."

"No, it's your turn now."

"Listen," says Ben, "I don't even feel cold, and you're shivering. You have a family, I'm single. You go next."

Rudy nods. There is no time to argue because he can see the swimmer sitting at the open doorway, feet dangling outside the air-craft, ready to be lowered.

Up in the cockpit, Aaron, well aware of how long everything is taking, speaks to Scott through his headset. "I'm going to try and help you guys by coming down in altitude to see if I can minimize your hoisting distance."

In an amazing display of control, the copilot lowers the aircraft into the trough, so the crest of the next approaching wave is higher than the helicopter. Aaron has found a rhythm. When the crest is about forty feet away, he increases altitude, lets it pass, and then lowers the helo back into the next trough. This simple but risky maneuver makes a world of difference for both Scott and Drew as the swimmer is lowered. Instead of Drew trailing forty feet behind the helicopter due to the wind, he is only about twenty aft, and Scott is able to time his descent into the water to coincide with the back side of a wave rather than the front, where it could break on him.

Scott manages to position Drew fifteen feet downwind from the raft. Drew releases and barely has to take a stroke; the raft is carried on a wave almost straight to him. Drew is thankful beyond words; he's dog-tired, and this allows him to conserve a little energy for the two remaining rescues, as well as the final hoist to get himself out of the watery chaos.

The swimmer puts an arm on the raft, spits out his snorkel, and says, "Okay, who's next?"

Ben points to Rudy. "He is."

"Okay," says Drew, "slide on out . . ." He has to pause, catch his breath, and let a wave of nausea pass. "I'll drag you away from the raft, and we'll wait for the basket."

Rudy watched the procedure with JP, so he knows what to do. He turns to Ben and says, "See you up there." Then he rolls out of the raft and lets Drew pull him a few feet away from the little vessel that has kept them alive against all odds. The basket is lowered within seconds, and Drew helps him inside it. Rudy now knows why two of them don't go up together; there is barely enough room for one.

Now that he's in the basket, the effects of hypothermia, stress, and exhaustion sweep down on him, enveloping him in bone-crushing weariness and stiffness. Maybe it's because he's in someone else's care, or maybe it's because he's no longer watching over JP, but whatever the reason, his body feels like it weighs a ton. He can sense the basket twisting and spinning, but he pays it no mind, too tired to even lift his head and look at the helicopter above him.

Scott is waiting at the door, working the pendant. When the basket arrives, he hauls it in. He's concerned about this survivor. The gray-bearded man struggles to get out of the basket, and when he does, he lands on all fours, with seawater pouring out of his foul-weather gear. Then he collapses on the cabin deck, rolling over on his back.

Scott is thinking heart attack. "Are you okay?" he shouts.

"Yes," gasps Rudy, "I'll be all right."

While Scott goes to work freeing Rudy from the inflatable life vest, JP, who has been sitting on the bench on the opposite wall, rallies and reaches out to his friend, helping remove the life vest, holding Rudy's shoulder as if unable to believe he's safe.

When they have the PFD off Rudy, he struggles to sit up, then collapses back into JP and Scott. The flight mechanic has his face inches from Rudy's, checking his breathing, searching his eyes.

"I'll be okay," says Rudy, "don't worry about me. Do your job."

Scott is thrilled to hear the survivor talking, making sense. He knows that precious seconds are ticking by, and he's feeling the strain of not knowing where Drew is, as well as their fuel constraints, when the bingo time demands that they leave.

Scott sees that Rudy cannot raise himself, and with a surge of pure power, the flight mechanic crouches, grabs Rudy under his right arm, and pulls him up and onto the bench next to JP.

With tears in his eyes, JP embraces Rudy. Both men never expected to be alive, never dreamed a rescue was possible. Whatever pain is shooting through JP's ribs is ignored as he holds his friend and says, "You made it, you made it."

While Rudy was being hoisted, the life raft carrying the last survivor has drifted far from the scene. Ben is alone, and four long minutes have gone by without a glimpse of the helicopter. Somehow the angry ocean seems more desolate, more menacing, making Ben feel forlorn and insignificant. He tries to stay positive, but he knows a number of different scenarios might have cropped up, making his rescue impossible. Ben's immediate concern, however, is hanging on to the life raft. With the other two men gone, the raft is much lighter and is surfing down waves at terrifying speeds. He's clutching the vessel's lifeline with all the strength he has. While he can't control what's happening with the helicopter, he knows he's as good as dead if he gets separated from the raft.

Drew is more than a couple hundred yards away from Ben, and although he is not with the raft, his position is the safer of the two. The helicopter is overhead, and the pilots aren't taking their eyes off him, positioning the aircraft so that Drew is always in sight.

Scott has moved the basket to a secure location in the cabin and attached the strop to the hook. "I'm lowering the strop," he announces to the pilots. "Go forward thirty feet."

Aaron moves the helo forward, waits for a wave crest to pass, and then lowers the steel bird into the trough.

Drew has no trouble swimming to the strop. He positions it around his chest and under his arms, then gives the thumbs-up sign. By prearrangement with Scott, they are going to air-taxi Drew to the raft in order to eliminate a complete hoisting and lowering of the swimmer. Drew can always change his mind and be returned to the helicopter simply by patting his head.

Scott retracts about forty feet of cable and tells the pilots that they can begin the search for the raft. Aaron brings the helo up another twenty feet and lets the wind slowly blow them backward. Drew is sailing a good thirty feet behind the helicopter and feels like he's moving at warp speed.

The rescue swimmer has no idea how long the hunt for the raft will take, so he tries to relax and visualize another successful survivor hoist. But the scene just below his flippers is too riveting to take his eyes off of. He cannot believe the size of the waves and is mesmerized by the way the wind snatches the top two feet of the crests and sends the spray and foam hurling through the air, far ahead of the roller itself. Sometimes the wind shifts a bit and peels back the top part of the wave, blowing it skyward. The waves range from fifty to seventy feet, with an occasional monster exceeding that. One colossal wave comes so close to Drew that he feels he could sit right down on the crest, and when it passes and he is dangling above the trough, it looks like the bottom of the canyon is a mile below him.

Drew sees the raft about the same time the rest of his crew does, and he shakes his head in wonder. *It looks like a surfboard! Scott will have to get me damn close.*

As soon as a wave crest passes beneath the raft, he can feel himself being lowered. He's not sure whether the helo is descending or if cable is being fed out. Whatever the technique, it works, because as the raft slides down into the next valley, Drew is only fifteen feet above it and downwind about twenty feet. *This is as close as they're going to get me.* Up come his arms, and he falls from the sling feet-first. As soon as he hits the water, he's sprinting to the raft. *I can't miss it. I've got to get it on this first try.* Like the pilots worrying about the helicopter's fuel, Drew is cognizant of his energy limits. He's been in the water or on the hook for about twenty minutes, and the swimming, grappling with the basket, and ingestion of seawater are taking a toll. If the speeding raft gets past him, he'll have to waste precious energy getting back in the strop and being lifted once again.

A breaking sea rolls him, and when Drew emerges from the turbulence, he's not sure where the raft is. He swivels around. *There it is! It's getting by me!* He puts his head down and kicks for all he's worth, intersecting the raft before it's gone.

Ben reaches out and holds on to Drew's harness. Drew, gasping for air, spits out the snorkel and holds on to the raft for a couple of seconds, gathering himself. "Okay!" he shouts to Ben. "Come out backward. But before we leave, I need to stab the raft!"

Ben gives Drew an incredulous look. Puncturing the raft means that if his hoist—or Drew's final hoist—fails, the raft will no longer be there as an emergency backup.

Despite his surprise, Ben slides from the raft and into the churning sea.

Drew pulls him in close and shouts in his ear, "I'm going to need my hands free! Grab on to my harness and hold on as tight as you can!" While he's talking, Drew feels something bump into his shoulder, and it's not Ben. The rescue swimmer is startled and spins around. Floating in the water is the malfunctioning GPIRB, which came free of its tether. Drew reaches out and grabs it, stuffing the mechanism in the pocket of his dry suit. He's not sure if it's working, but he doesn't want to chance an emergency device giving off a signal for a rescue that's already done. That line of reasoning is why he's going to sink the raft. If the raft somehow managed to stay afloat for another couple of days, it's possible that a ship would spot it and a whole new rescue might be launched.

Reaching into a pocket on his vest, Drew withdraws his knife, first stabbing the raft, then using a sweeping motion to put a big slice in it. The raft deflates, though part of it stays on the surface. Drew locks one arm around Ben and tows him a few feet away, using his free arm to motion to Scott for the basket.

Ben is the heaviest of the three survivors, and Drew is nearing total exhaustion when the basket arrives. He's relieved when Ben crawls inside the basket with little help, then alarmed when Ben crouches with his hands on the bails. Drew shouts, "Sit down and keep your knees up by your chest."

Ben can't hear a word he is saying now that the helicopter is directly overhead.

Drew tries a different approach. He motions for Ben to sit while at the same time hitting the back of the survivor's knees, which forces him to go down. Ben now understands and gives Drew a thumbs-up as he is carried skyward, leaving the rescue swimmer alone in the ocean.

Scott uses his left arm to push the cable as far away from the aircraft as possible while it slowly retracts through his gloved hand. He suddenly stops the hoist. Frayed strands of cable have sliced through his glove, just missing his skin. With the jerking motion of the helicopter, it's hard to see how many strands have broken free. He's processing the problem as fast as he can, knowing that cutting the cable above the frayed section and reattaching a new cable will take far too long. Scott is not worried that the frayed cable will break but that it may get balled up and stuck in the hoist. He makes a quick decision and resumes the hoist, calculating—and praying—that the cable will make both this hoist and the final one for Drew.

CHAPTER TWENTY-FIVE

HE'S GOING TO DROWN

Against all odds, the final survivor is being hoisted to safety. Ben isn't wild about heights, and he grips the basket with all his strength, surprised by how thin the cable is that supports him. As he nears the helicopter and the deafening *thock-thock-thock* of its rotors, he thinks the basket looks like it will be drawn right into the steel underside of the aircraft.

JP, sitting against the wall opposite the cabin door, is thinking clearly now, in part due to the warmth of the cabin. He has no idea that Ben is on his way up, and he senses that something has gone wrong because several minutes have gone by since Rudy was retrieved. He's worried sick that Ben won't make it, and he feels responsible, going back over every decision he made, second-guessing himself, cursing the GPIRB that went dead. He's startled out of his ruminations when the basket carrying Ben is at the door.

Scott guides the basket inside, and Ben gets a leg out and rolls onto the floor. JP and Rudy reach out, tapping his head, patting his shoulder repeatedly, as if to make sure it's really him and not a hallucination. Ben sits facing his friends and gives them a quick thumbs-up, a surprised look on his face, not quite believing he is out of the raft and up in the sky.

Roller after giant roller slides under the rescue swimmer, who is vomiting violently, his body trying to rid itself of the seawater he has ingested. Drew faces the awful truth that all his laps in the pool, weight lifting, ocean simulated rescues, and various other forms of training have made him stronger and tougher than other humans but no match for waves of this magnitude. He's been exerting himself nonstop for almost half an hour, and he's spent. Over and over he tells himself, *Just hang on for a couple more minutes.* But time has lost its normal progression, and seconds feel like minutes, minutes like hours.

Then disaster. A giant wave breaks directly on the swimmer, driving him down while he has his mouth open in the act of vomiting. He can feel himself ingesting more seawater, coughing and choking as he tumbles inside the maw of the wave. He claws at the water, trying to propel his body in the direction he thinks is the surface. *Air, air,* his brain screams.

Prior to this comber, Aaron and Nevada had been making sure they never lose sight of Drew, alarmed by the beating the rescue swimmer is taking. During the rescues, Drew was mostly on the surface, riding the waves like a kid on a roller coaster. But the two pilots noticed that once the rescues were complete, their swimmer was disappearing underwater every time a wave broke anywhere near him. And it seemed that when he popped back up, he barely had time to grab a breath before foam engulfed him.

Aaron is thinking, *This is bad, he's going to drown right in front of us.* He then watches in horror as the house-sized wave avalanches on the swimmer. White water swirls in all directions. There is no sign of Drew.

Aaron holds his breath, craning forward to spot Drew's neon helmet. *Come on, come on,* a desperate Aaron urges, *you can do it,* trying to will his swimmer to the surface.

Drew breaks through the churning water. He gulps in a mix of foam and air, frantically waving his arm back and forth over his head, the emergency signal. He's got nothing left, he's got to get out of the water, knowing he won't survive another wave like that.

Aaron sees Drew first. "I'm getting the emergency signal!" shouts the copilot. "I'm moving closer."

Scott, who is disconnecting the basket from the hook, can't believe his ears. In all his many rescues, this has never happened, and Drew is the toughest swimmer he's ever worked with. Adrenaline surges into every muscle of the flight mechanic's body, and he tells himself, *Stay calm, no mistakes.*

Technically, the rule is to lower the basket if a swimmer is in trouble. But Scott decides against it, thinking that Drew might have cramped up and may not be able to climb inside. And the basket, being much larger than the bare hook, will be blown far aft by the eighty-knot winds and will take longer to position close to Drew.

Scott has forgotten all about the frayed strands of the cable and starts lowering the hook, conning the pilots into the correct position to get as close as possible to Drew. Once again the flight mechanic is on his stomach, his head and shoulders outside the aircraft. The wind continues to make it hard for him to get a decent breath of air. Whenever he needs to tell the pilots anything, he's got to turn his head to the side, away from the cold blasts. He's running through different scenarios if Drew can't get himself attached to the hook. He could try the strop but knows that will waste more time because of the way it will sail in the wind. Another option, and not a good one, is to lower the basket and try to scoop Drew up. If Drew becomes unconscious, the success of this maneuver is unlikely. But if these options don't work, there are no more. The swimmer will die.

Drew is treading water, watching the hook descend, hoping he won't have to swim more than a couple of strokes to it, not knowing for sure what his body is capable of at this point. With relief, he sees how Scott and the pilots have worked the helo so that the hook is within five feet, and he manages a couple kicks of his flipper, grabbing the hook with his right hand. He attaches it to the ring in the front of his harness located near the bottom of his rib cage. Then he notices that the harness leg straps are high up around his butt rather than around his middle thigh. *I've got to move these down . . . if a wave falls out from under me, I'm going to take the brunt of it on my back.*

A second or two later, as Drew struggles with the straps, a wave crest passes beneath him. There is almost no slack in the cable, so he doesn't slide down the back of the wave. Instead, without the water to support his body, he is yanked so violently that his head and back jerk backward and he feels like he has been snapped in two. A sharp white-hot pain shoots up his back, and he moans in agony. The cable is bringing him higher, but instead of coming up in a sitting position, he has his belly at the highest point and his back arched in an awkward position. He flails his arms, trying to grab the front of his harness or the hook, anything to sit up before his back breaks.

• • •

Scott saw that the wave crest was catching Drew unaware, and the flight mechanic paid out cable as fast as he could. But not fast enough. He watched in horror as Drew was jerked so suddenly that his back bent like a gymnast's and his head almost touched his flippers. The helicopter actually shuddered from the weight of Drew's fall.

"Oh no!" cries Scott. Then a five-second pause. "I might have broken his back."

Aaron hears this comment through his headset, and a cold chill races up his spine. *Did I just hear that right?* He glances at Nevada, whose face is ashen. Nevada starts to say something to Scott, then thinks better of it. The pilots can't stand the tension, feel like jumping out of their skin, because there is not a damn thing they can do. It's all up to Scott and Drew. Adding to their stress is the fact that Drew is directly below the aircraft, and neither pilot can see him.

Scott's right hand is pressing the pendant while the retracting cable slides through his gloved left hand. He can feel where the frayed cable strands are sticking out, and he's holding his breath, hoping the hoist mechanism doesn't jam when the loose ends are pulled through. None of this is in the script; Scott feels like everything is going all wrong and they are on the verge of disaster. The lift seems to be happening in slow motion. Scott is trying to see Drew's face, wondering if he is conscious. A million thoughts race through Scott's mind, but the dominant one is: *If his back is broken, I'll never forgive myself.*

Scott gets the swimmer to the door and hauls him in. Drew collapses on the floor. Scott shouts, "Are you okay? Are you okay?"

Drew can't talk but tries to nod. He's having trouble breathing, and his back is spasming. He looks up and sees the three survivors staring at him, and his training starts to kick in. As the aircraft's emergency medical technician he has to look after the survivors, and he knows one of them has broken ribs. He strains to sit up.

"Drew!" shouts Scott. "Lie back down!"

"I'm fine."

"No, you're not fine, I saw what happened. Let me get you a neck brace."

Drew somehow manages to sit up and slides toward JP. He puts an oxygen mask on the injured survivor. He leans toward JP and shouts in his ear, "Are you okay?" Then he checks on the other two survivors.

The pilots are blasting the heat, but Drew is chilled. There is a considerable amount of water inside his dry suit—both sweat and ocean—and it's making him shiver. He's light-headed and woozy and moves toward the closed cabin door. He takes a sip of water and immediately feels nauseated and knows he's going to be sick again. He can feel the bile rising, and not wanting to stink up the cabin, he grabs one of his flippers and pukes in it. Then he opens a small six-inch hatch in the cabin door and dumps the contents. When he turns around, the survivors are staring at him again, and Scott is shaking his head. Drew manages a weak smile and then tries to lie down, but the contractions in his back make straightening out impossible, so he sits facing the survivors, wondering if he's going to pass out.

Scott moves over to Drew and starts apologizing for not being able to let out enough cable. Drew stops him in midsentence. "Listen," says the rescue swimmer, "you got me out. That's all that matters."

CHAPTER TWENTY-SIX

THE *ILLUSION*

While the helicopter carrying Ben, Rudy, and JP is speeding toward land, another helo is racing out to sea. There are still two sailboats in distress: the *Flying Colours* and the *Illusion,* both over two hundred miles out in the Gulf Stream, southwest of where the *Sean Seamour II* went down. A C-130 that had been searching for the *Flying Colours* was diverted to the *Illusion* when SAR Headquarters received its EPIRB signal around midmorning. The C-130 quickly located the vessel and is circling on-scene until the helicopter arrives.

The sixty-seven-foot aluminum-hulled *Illusion* had left Grand Bahama Island on May 3, bound for Newport, Rhode Island. Captain Chris Leitch and crew members James Coates and Jessica Youngblood were delivering the boat to new owners. The sailors had enjoyed two days of smooth sailing until they ran into building seas southeast of Cape Hatteras. The winds became too much for their sails, and they switched to engine power, prepared to ride out what they thought would be a minor storm. It wasn't long before the engine inexplicably lost power. Leitch, like JP, did not want to be caught in the Gulf Stream if the storm continued to grow in strength, so he raised a bit of sail and slowly pounded to the east, toward the *Sean Seamour II* and the *Flying Colours*.

The storm was too big to outrun, and the *Illusion*'s anchor came loose and started banging against the hull, eventually piercing it. The vessel started taking on water, shorting out power to their bilge pump. To make matters worse, there was no life raft, leaving the captain no choice but to send out a Mayday.

• • •

The Jayhawk HH-60 helicopter heading to the *Illusion* is commanded by Scott Walden, accompanied by Copilot Bill Coty, Flight Mechanic Justin Cimbak, and Rescue Swimmer Steve Fischer. The crew had already made one flight earlier that morning, when they sped toward the coordinates of the *Flying Colours* EPIRB signal. Two factors caused them to turn back toward land: Visibility was terrible, and the C-130 on-scene had not found so much as a seat cushion. Walden knew that the EPIRB hit was at the outer edge of his helicopter's fuel capacity and that he would not be able to conduct both a search and a rescue. He decided to fly to Smith Field in Morehead City, North Carolina (closer to the EPIRB hit than Elizabeth City), refuel, and be ready when the vessel or survivors were located.

The helo crew had been waiting at Smith Field for about three hours when SAR Headquarters told Walden to gather his crew and launch. The commander assumed the *Flying Colours* had been sighted and was surprised to learn that he was being sent to a different vessel, the *Illusion*. The C-130 had not only located the *Illusion* but had established radio communication with the captain.

Now airborne, Commander Walden decides to fly at a low altitude for better visibility and less turbulence. Copilot Bill Coty is in the right seat and Walden in the left. They speed in and out of bands of pouring rain and sustained winds of sixty knots, but what catches the attention of the crew is the state of the ocean below. It resembles a mountain range, with snowcapped peaks and deep valleys. Coty wonders if the seas will be too much for the rescue swimmer and hoist operator to effectively extract the survivors. Rescue swimmer Steve Fischer has similar thoughts: *Looks like a washing machine; this will be my toughest rescue yet.* He has butterflies in his stomach and gets himself in the right frame of mind by saying to himself, *This is real. You've got to do this perfectly.* It is probably a blessing that he has no idea what swimmer Drew Dazzo went through in his rescue.

Fischer has been a rescue swimmer for three years and has done what he thinks of as small SAR cases, such as medevacs and hoisting people who became stranded on sandbars. Each had its dangers, but nothing like what he'll face here. He knows that once he unhooks from the cable in the chaos below, he's on his own, and the lives of the three people on the sailboat will be squarely on his shoulders. Now he glances at the charging waves and thinks, *Thank God it's daylight. There's no way we could do this at night.*

To save time when they arrive, Walden asks the on-scene C-130 to radio the *Illusion*'s captain and review the steps the rescue swimmer will take to get them off the boat and safely in the helicopter. The C-130 reports back to the commander with both good and bad news: On-scene conditions are the worst he has ever seen, but the captain is knowledgeable, and all three crew members are in survival suits.

Coty listens in and is relieved to know the survivors will be as ready as they can be. Just knowing they are alive is a plus. He's done missions where people were facedown in the water when he arrived, and the rescue became a body recovery.

When they arrive above the *Illusion,* it looks like a toy, rolling and lurching from side to side, its mast sometimes so far over that it looks like it will touch the ocean. Walden establishes contact with the captain, Chris Leitch, and stresses that when the rescue swimmer instructs the first survivor to jump, the other two crew members must stay on the boat. Multiple people in the water mean multiple headaches, and Walden is aware of too many cases where survivors in the water got separated. In these seas, that means death. He also knows that once a person is in the water, getting back on the boat is not an option—the boat's freeboard makes it a big target for the wind and pushes it faster than a person can swim.

Walden gives the captain more instructions. "I want you to tie about twenty to thirty feet of line to a life ring and throw it off the side of the boat. That way, if the person jumping off the boat is not immediately grabbed by the rescue swimmer, he'll have something to hang on to."

Swimmer Steve Fischer listens in on the conversation, then removes his headset and puts on his neon-yellow helmet, mask, and flippers. Flight Mechanic Cimbak is crouched by the door, and the swimmer slides over and gets hooked up. The two men have formulated a plan in which they will lower Fischer on the hook, but he will also have the strop for the first survivor. They want to do a direct deployment whereby Fischer has the survivor jump when he reaches the water. Fischer hopes to stay on the hook while putting the survivor in the strop and then be hoisted together.

Cimbak lowers Fischer, and the swimmer's first surprise happens just a few feet from the water. He gets zapped by static electricity. He lets out a yell and is stunned for a couple seconds. The steel hook is like a magnet for the electricity, and it could have been far worse. (A rescue swimmer being lowered to an oil tanker once got an electrical shock so strong that a filling came out of one of his teeth.)

Fischer's second surprise occurs when he enters the water and motions for the first survivor, Jessica Youngblood, to jump. As soon as she's in the ocean, the waves catch her and carry her away so fast that she's beyond the rescue swimmer's grasp. Now Fischer is zapped in a different way: Adrenaline shoots through his body, and his heart races. If he loses sight of her in the foam, he'll have a hard time finding her again. He immediately unclips from the hook and is off to the races, kicking and stroking harder than he ever has in his life. He is at her side in seconds.

Cimbak realizes the strop at the end of the hook is blowing far aft of the helo and decides the basket will work better for Fischer. He retrieves the hook and strop, then attaches the basket and lowers it to the rescue swimmer. Once the survivor is in the basket, he brings her up without incident.

The waves sweep Fischer far from both the helo and the sailboat. One of his training sessions flashes through his mind. While at advanced rescue swimmer school, he was dropped in the ocean by a helicopter and left there for two hours alone. It was a sobering reminder of what it feels like if you can't get back to the helo, but it also taught him about the kind of steady patience needed. He knows that when you're alone in the ocean, time crawls, so now he just tries to relax and conserve energy—not an easy thing to do when every third or fourth wave is driving him under.

When Fischer is lifted back up to the helo, he pukes out the seawater, then he and Cimbak decide to use the strop again so the swimmer isn't pummeled by the waves for long. But when he's lowered, he again can't get close enough to the survivor, who jumps. Fischer releases from the hook and fights his way to the sailor, then they wait for the basket and repeat the first rescue.

It isn't until the third and final rescue that Fischer is able to snatch the survivor the minute he jumps. He puts the strop around him, and they go up together, which is a big relief for the swimmer, who avoids the pummeling while waiting in the water.

With everyone safely in the aircraft, the survivors are high-fiving and thanking the Coast Guard men for saving their lives as the pilots head the helo for land. The flight will take almost twice as long because they are buffeted by headwinds, but the aircraft crew is feeling good about what they have accomplished. Then Coty smells smoke. "Do you smell that?" he asks Walden.

"Sure do. Let's go through the checklist."

While they troubleshoot, Coty's first thought is of the C-130. He's glad that it's escorting them. If they have to ditch, and if they survive—a big if—at least the C-130 will be on-scene and can drop life rafts and circle until another helicopter arrives.

Putting the aircraft down in the water would be a last resort, and only if the helo catches fire or if the smoke in the cockpit becomes so thick that they can't fly. Should it come to ditching, the pilots' first act would be to get the helicopter near the ocean and in a hover so the survivors could be lowered by the hook or jump out and into the water. The rescue swimmer and flight mechanic would go next, and finally, the copilot. The pilot would then move the aircraft away from those in the water before putting it down. His survival would be questionable, depending on the force of the impact and whether he could exit safely when the rotors flipped it upside down.

The pilots complete the checklist and everything is looking good. They are perplexed but relieved that no major malfunction is occurring and that the smoke is not getting worse. Then Coty remembers that this particular helo had a smoke problem several weeks earlier that was attributed to a faulty heater. He shuts off the heater, and the incoming smoke diminishes before stopping. Not wanting to take any chances, Walden decides to land at the closest airfield, which is back in Morehead City, North Carolina.

When they arrive, all are relieved, especially the sailors. Jessica Youngblood shakes Fischer's hand and says, "Thank you, and my mother thanks you!"

A STORM TOO SOON

Walden and his crew want to rest, but the wind starts to kick up on land. The commander determines that it is safe to fly with the heater off, and he decides that they'd better get the helicopter back to Elizabeth City before night closes in. There is one last boat in trouble, the *Flying Colours,* and the crew figures it won't be long before they are sent back out to the moving mountains of the Gulf Stream.

CHAPTER TWENTY-SEVEN

THE *FLYING COLOURS* AND CHERRY POINT NAVAL HOSPITAL

It's hard for those of us in a comfortable setting to fully understand the psychological trauma that has enveloped Ben, Rudy, and JP. First there was the nerve-wracking buildup of the waves battering the boat, hitting so hard that they boomed upon impact. That was followed by the first capsizing, which sent the men ricocheting through the cabin and colliding into one another. Then the GPIRB failed, followed by the second capsizing, after which the boat did not immediately right itself. This was when JP, with broken ribs, swam out of the boat, found the life raft pinned by the spreader, and managed to free it, receiving more cracked ribs for his effort. Next came the boarding of the raft and the terrifying ride down massive waves that sometimes pitched the shell-shocked men into the sea. They lived through a nightmare few have endured, and the surreal experience has left them numb.

Now, flying toward land, the three sailors are each lost in his thoughts. They don't feel like talking, but even if they did, they couldn't be heard over the whine of the engine and the roar of the rotors. JP is in pain, shivering, and exhausted. The turbulence isn't helping his ribs, and the sleep-deprived captain just wants to be on dry land. He is claustrophobic inside the helicopter, which reminds him of being inside a submarine and how, when the hatch closed, he felt entombed. He wonders how he will break the news to his wife. It's too much to think about. He steels himself for the hour-and-forty-five-minute ride back to the U.S.

His one diversion during the flight is staring at copilot Aaron Nelson, who has barely moved. Even during the rescues of Ben and Rudy, JP noticed that Aaron used the subtlest of touches to deftly make the helicopter move left or right or change altitude. He wonders how in the world the copilot has kept such focus and concentration for so long.

His beloved *Sean Seamour II* is at the bottom of the ocean, but JP is riding a wave of relief from seeing Rudy and Ben rescued. He mistakenly thought the swimmer was too exhausted to do any more after his own rescue, and he'd begun to panic at the thought that his two crewmates would be left in the storm.

Nevada is so proud of his crew that he needs a moment before he says anything. He composes himself and gets on the radio to the C-130 escorting them back, giving them a complete update, knowing their concern about Drew's welfare. He tells Commander Beavis in the C-130 that he marked the position when they got on-scene and did the same when they picked up Drew. "We moved one point eight miles in twenty-eight minutes. That's how fast the raft was moving."

Aaron, who may look to JP like a programmed robot, is anything but. He is roasting in his dry suit. During the rescue, he had as much adrenaline coursing through his body as Drew and Scott, but no way to burn it off. Now the heavy, sick feeling that often follows a burst of adrenaline is setting in, and he begins to feel nauseated. "Take the controls," he says to Nevada. "I'm not doing well."

Once Nevada takes over, Aaron slumps in his seat. His head hangs, and he tries not to throw up. He opens a little round air scoop in the lower portion of the Plexiglas window and bends all the way forward, letting the fresh air blow on his face, hoping for the nausea to pass. When it doesn't, he starts looking for something to vomit in and eyes the helmet bag by his seat. The whole time he's thinking, *How hot do these survivors have to be.*

Rather than fly back to Elizabeth City, Nevada has decided to save time by going to Marine Corps Air Station Cherry Point. When they are within seventy-five miles of land, the C-130 peels off and heads back out to sea to search for the *Flying Colours*. Aaron starts to wonder if they, too, will be sent back out.

Nevada, thinking the same thing, says, "If we go back out, I can fly and look for that other EPIRB hit. We can get hot gas [refuel while the engine is running] and be ready in no time."

"I don't think we're going back out," says Aaron. "I'm still not doing so well."

Then the two men remember the frayed cable and realize they would have to fly to Elizabeth City to get it replaced and pick up a new rescue swimmer.

"You're right," says Nevada, "let's shut it down. You guys did a great job."

Cherry Point has been alerted to the injuries aboard the helicopter, and when they land, three ambulances race up to the aircraft as the pilots power it down.

Scott opens the cabin door and tells Ben, who is closest to the opening, to exit first. EMTs escort him to an ambulance, despite his protests that he is fine. Rudy, who has been shivering from exposure, is next. He, too, says he doesn't need to go to the hospital. But when he steps out of the helicopter, he has trouble standing. Paramedics move in and support him, then hustle him into the ambulance, where they strip off his wet clothes and wrap him in blankets with heat packs pressed against his body. They take his temperature, and it is 95 degrees—not life-threatening, but still low, considering he was in the helo for over an hour and a half with the heater blasting.

JP comes out next, and the paramedics get him on a special board for neck and back injuries. In the ambulance, a female EMT starts to remove his clothes. When JP protests, she says, "Don't worry, I've seen it before, and besides—after you being in the cold water, there's nothing to see." For the first time in two days, JP smiles. His core temperature is about the same as Rudy's, and the medics put hot pads against his skin and cover him in blankets.

Scott helps Drew to the doorway. The paramedics place him on the special board and hustle him into one of the ambulances, where they cut off his dry suit. As they hook Drew up to an IV, Scott pokes his head inside the ambulance and pats his friend on the shoulder, still feeling that the last hoist might have ended Drew's career.

With the rescue of the sailors from the *Seeker,* the *Sean Seamour II,* and the *Illusion* completed, the Coast Guard is utilizing all its resources in the quest to find the *Flying Colours*. A C-130 has been searching for the last hour and is now joined by a second C-130, but not a trace of the boat can be seen. The coordinates from the vessel's EPIRB were about 160 nautical miles southeast of Cape Lookout, North Carolina. Although the *Flying Colours* EPIRB was activated shortly after JP's, the signal abruptly stopped about seven a.m. The Coast Guard is using computer models to estimate how far and in which direction the vessel might have drifted.

The fifty-four-foot single-mast *Flying Colours* had a crew of four: thirty-nine-year-old Captain Patrick Topping; thirty-four-year-old Jason Franks; twenty-six-year-old Christine Grinavic; and twenty-two-year-old Rhiannon Borisoff. The foursome left St. Thomas, U.S. Virgin Islands, on April 30 and were delivering the boat, as instructed by its owners, to Annapolis, Maryland. Both Patrick Topping and Jason Franks were experienced sailors and held captain's licenses and had logged many sailing miles on a variety of boats. Christine Grinavic and Rhiannon Borisoff also had sailing experience; Grinavic had worked as a crew member on a luxury yacht, the *Arabella,* and had made voyages from Newport, Rhode Island, to the Virgin Islands.

The vessel, a Hinckley yacht built in 1992, did have an eight-man life raft on board. Spotters in the C-130s are searching for the raft or the vessel and are puzzled that, with a relatively good location fix, they are unable to spot either. In the late afternoon a Jayhawk joins the C-130s on the scene, and the cutter *Tampa* continues its slow progress into the storm to assist with the search. Meanwhile, at SAR Headquarters, calls are made to various area ports in hopes that the blue-and-white *Flying Colours* has found safe harbor. But no one has seen the vessel, and the families of the sailors begin an agonizing wait for any positive news.

Rudy, Ben, JP, and Drew are all in separate rooms at the Cherry Point naval hospital. Rudy is being treated on a machine for hypothermia while his clothing is washed and dried and his passport and wallet are spread out to dry. His back aches, but the pain is manageable. Ben is feeling fine, but he's wondering how in the world he will get home to England. He didn't think to grab his passport and wallet when the boat was sinking—he didn't expect he'd be alive to use them—and now he feels a bit like he doesn't exist, as if he's in a bizarre dream.

JP, surprisingly, refuses X-rays on his broken ribs, fearing they'll mean an overnight stay in the hospital. (Later X-rays show that ten of his ribs are broken.) Instead, he accepts a strong painkiller. Between the medication and the relief that his crew is okay, he feels high, even a bit strong.

Drew's back is being X-rayed for possible cracked vertebrae; fortunately, his injury is strained muscles rather than a broken back. Doctors ask if he needs morphine, and the swimmer declines but does take strong painkillers. He then rests in bed with the curtains drawn until a nurse tells him that his wife is on the phone. He's surprised that she tracked him down so quickly and even more startled by the emotion that wells up in him when he hears her voice. Tears roll down his face, and for a moment he is unable to talk.

Later, he tries getting out of bed. He shuffles over to the nurses' station, where a nurse asks how his back is feeling. Drew answers, "It's better, and I'm finally starting to warm up."

"Well," says the nurse, "those other guys are starting to warm up, too."

"What other guys?"

"The three who came off the helicopter with you."

Drew is taken aback. He had no idea the survivors are at the same hospital. "You're kidding!" he exclaims. "Can I go see them?"

"Sure, they're all together in one room, having something to eat."

When Drew enters the room, he sees the three men sitting in chairs with a space heater blasting. "Pull up a chair," says Ben.

Over the next hour, the survivors tell Drew what happened to them on the sailboat and in the raft prior to his arrival. They explain the knockdown, how JP broke his ribs, the length of time they spent in the upside-down boat, the way they abandoned ship, and finally, their time in and out of the life raft, with no hope that help was coming.

As Drew listens, he reflects that what he went through was minor compared to this story. He hangs on every word; normally, once the survivors leave the helicopter, he never sees them again. The swimmer is awed by what these three men endured but also by their even-keeled spirit, considering what they have gone through.

Nevada, Aaron, and Scott have flown back to Elizabeth City, where the media is waiting for them. Scott and Aaron duck out and leave Nevada alone to answer questions. When he is finished, he walks into the Operations Center and describes the mission, and other pilots think he's exaggerating about the waves. "Ask Drew, Scott, and Aaron, they'll confirm it. Aaron and I both saw the altimeter swing more than seventy feet. We got some video we can show you later."

Scott knows another crew will use the helicopter to look for the *Flying Colours,* so the first thing he does is alert the mechanics in Maintenance Control to the frayed strands on the cable. A mechanic gets to work but soon walks over to Scott and says, "I checked the cable, and it's fine."

"How far did you run it out?"

"Fifty feet."

"Run it out a hundred feet."

The mechanic looks at Scott like he's lost his mind. Hoists are normally done within fifty feet of the water. But this wasn't a normal mission. With waves topping seventy feet, the helicopter was usually at an altitude of ninety to a hundred feet to avoid being taken out by a wave.

Sure enough, after the mechanic extracts a hundred feet of cable, the frayed strands are clearly visible. The entire cable is replaced.

Next Scott walks over to the C-130 crew and shakes their hands, saying a simple thank-you. Then he heads home. He doesn't feel elated but keeps replaying over and over how he let Drew fall off the wave.

Aaron heads straight home after taking off his gear, still feeling ill. His wife, who doesn't know about the extreme conditions he flew into, says, "You're home earlier than I thought."

Aaron nods. He feels like he has been gone for a week. He then lies down on the living room floor.

"What's the matter?" asks his wife with alarm in her voice.

Aaron doesn't know where to start. He massages his temples.

Then he begins, "I've just seen some of the most amazing and crazy things of my life." He explains the giant seas, the hurricane-force winds, and the three men in the raft. When he describes what happened to Drew and how worried he was that they wouldn't get him back in the helo, he chokes up, surprised by the emotion pouring out.

At the end of the story, images of what happened keep flickering through his mind. Then he falls asleep, right there on the living room floor.

CHAPTER TWENTY-EIGHT

HEADING HOME

JP's stepmother can finally rest easy. Geoff Pagels at SAR Headquarters continually updated her and let her know that all three sailors on the *Sean Seamour II* were rescued. Later, JP calls Betty and says he's okay, electing not to tell her about the broken ribs or how lucky he is to be alive.

"Can I call Mayke?" Betty asked.

"Yes. I can't call overseas from here. Just tell her I'm okay and not to worry."

Betty immediately dials Mayke in France, but when she picks up the phone, Betty hesitates, not sure how to begin.

"Hi Mayke, it's Betty. How are you?

Mayke, who had the vision of the boat in trouble, quickly asks, "What's the matter?"

Betty pauses. "Are you sitting down?" She hears Mayke take a deep breath. Betty plows ahead. "Listen, JP is fine. But the boat is gone. There was a terrible storm."

"I knew it, I knew it!" cries Mayke. "I had those terrible dreams."

The two women talk a while longer, with Betty passing along what she learned from Geoff Pagels and JP. "JP will call you as soon as he is able," says Betty in closing. "He's going to be released from the hospital any minute and will probably come here to Cape Cod."

After Mayke hangs up, she stares out the window. She is relieved that her husband is physically okay, but she feels ill over the loss of the boat and the ordeal's impact on JP. He spent countless hours working on the vessel, improving it in a myriad of ways, and he had many personal items on board. She knows its loss will be a bitter blow, but she's more concerned about what happened to her husband in the storm, what trauma he will try and hide from her.

The three survivors are released from the hospital and given spending money from the Red Cross: enough for food, lodging, and transportation on their trek back into the land-based world. While the clothes the men had on in the water—pants and shirts—are being cleaned, they head to the PX at Cherry Point in their hospital gowns, picking out the bare necessities, such as underwear and socks. JP purchases a pair of shoes and decides to keep the box to use as his "luggage," thinking how, in twenty-four hours, he has gone from captain of a beautiful vessel to captain of a shoe box. He still can't get his head around what happened; his emotions bounce between numbness to a sensation that the last two days didn't really happen and he will wake up from the nightmare. *How can it be that a storm of this magnitude wasn't forecast well in advance, and how can it be that a state-of-the-art GPIRB, which was just professionally recertified, died after an hour and a half.* He wants to replay everything that happened, but he is so sleep-deprived that he decides now is not the time, just wanting to get through the rest of the day.

After getting dressed, they're driven to a Days Inn, and the man behind the counter asks if they have luggage. JP points to his shoe box. After checking into the hotel, the three men walk across the street and enter a restaurant. As they are ushered to a table by a waitress, all three men look up at a television mounted on the wall. A news reporter is explaining that there is a major storm offshore and the Coast Guard rescued nine people from three different sailboats. A fourth sailboat is missing. The reporter says that three of the survivors were found in a damaged life raft being battered by seventy-foot seas.

"Those are some lucky guys," says the waitress. "I wonder what kind of shape they're in."

"Well, those guys are us," says Ben.

The waitress's jaw drops. She stares at the men, then stammers, "You're serious, aren't you?"

Rudy nods.

"Well," says the waitress, "drinks are on the house."

As they listen to the broadcast, JP hears the reporter referring to a vessel named the *Lou Pantai*. *Why are they calling the* Sean Seamour II *by the name of my old boat, and how do they even know its name?* Again he wants to think it through, but he's too tired to tackle the puzzle.

Over dinner, the three men discuss how they will get home. They won't be able to take a plane because neither Ben nor JP has identification. Rudy has his driver's license, so they decide to rent a car and drive to Washington, D.C., where Ben can hopefully get help at the British embassy and JP at the French embassy. Having been a consultant to the French government, JP knows they have him registered and is confident that he can get the paperwork for his trip back to France and Mayke.

The next morning they rent a van rather than a car so they can stretch out. They are still exhausted, and each man needs his space as they all come to grips with what has happened. As they begin the long drive, they hear on the radio that after twenty-four hours of searching, the *Flying Colours* crew has not been found. The announcer explains that the Coast Guard has mounted a massive search by air and water, that the storm has abated, and that searchers are hopeful they will find the crew with better visibility. The three men in the van are pessimistic. Only they know what it was like to be in the water and in a raft for hours in punishing waves. They surmise that if the crew hasn't been rescued by now, the missing sailors either will be found dead or went down with the boat. It causes the three survivors great anguish to even think about others being in the same predicament. Already someone has said to Rudy, "God saved you," and Rudy thinks, *We were just lucky. God certainly didn't choose us over the four young people on the* Flying Colours.

As they drive north, approaching Elizabeth City, they decide to call the air station and arrange to personally thank the pilots and the hoist operator who saved their lives. They learn that the men are not on duty, so they push on, resolving to write to the rescuers when they get home.

When they near Annapolis, the terrible throbbing in JP's chest worsens, no matter how many painkillers he takes. Rudy, who is driving, is having back spasms that make him miserable. They stop at the first hotel they see and spend the night. The next morning they arrive in Washington, D.C., and after long waits at the embassies, both Ben and JP receive the necessary paperwork to get home. Both men are relieved—at least they have something to prove they exist, that they are not illegal aliens or terrorists. And JP has his first new item to put in the shoe box.

They continue driving north, staying the night in Newark, New Jersey, before bringing Ben to JFK International Airport, where he says goodbye. They talk about sailing, and JP promises a cruise in the Mediterranean, but Ben wonders if he will ever see his friends again. He is numb from the ordeal, wondering about all the many twists and turns that either caused the calamity or helped them survive. As the plane takes off, Ben stares out into the ocean. *What would have happened if I hadn't just bought that knife we used to cut the raft free of the boat? What about JP finding the strength to swim out of the overturned boat and free the raft from the mast? What if Rudy hadn't grabbed some flares as the boat was going down? What if . . .* Then he stops. There are just too many what-ifs. The things that kept them alive were the result of good decisions, luck, and maybe fate.

Rudy and JP drive directly to Betty's house on Cape Cod. Betty notices how quiet the two men are and how reluctant they are to talk about what they have been through. It's obvious to her that JP is in a lot of pain, but he's also got a faraway look in his eyes, and she knows he's reliving what happened, going over every step. He asks her what the Coast Guard said when they first called her, and she explains they asked if she knew whether the sailboat *Lou Pantai* was out at sea.

Then it hits JP. It was the old EPIRB, the one that was swept clear of the boat during the first knockdown, that saved their life. His mind is spinning. *What about the signal from the new GPIRB? Its light showed that it was on for an hour and a half before it died.* This marks the beginning of JP's quest to find out what really happened.

The next morning Rudy says he will begin his drive to Ottawa. Both Betty and JP try to convince him to rest another night, but Rudy wants to be moving.

JP walks Rudy to the van. Each saved the other man's life several times in those desperate hours in the capsized boat and tattered life raft. Now they are at a loss for words. They simply embrace, then say goodbye, knowing they will have to deal with the aftermath of the experience on their own. It won't be easy.

EPILOGUE

No trace of the *Flying Colours* was ever found. A short biography of the four sailors on board, written by their families, follows this epilogue.

JEAN PIERRE DE LUTZ (JP)

JP's lifelong dream and personal challenge to circumnavigate the globe was over, crushed by a storm too soon. That same storm, however, tested him in a multitude of ways, some more severe than might have happened on a solo circumnavigation. He met the trials that the storm tossed at him by enduring, outlasting, and pushing ahead, just as he did as a boy after his father dumped the pot of boiling water on him.

The aftermath of an event like the one JP went through in the Gulf Stream can be as brutal as the storm itself. During the emergency he was in a fight and action was required, in some cases with no time for deliberation. He had to first swim out of the overturned boat in the darkness, then get under the broken mast to lift the spreader, and finally, heave the raft from windward to the lee of the vessel. It took courage and fighting through the pain of broken ribs. It was survival: Do whatever you can to avoid drowning.

Back on land, the steps to move forward were not as clear. The threats to JP's well-being were not external but internal. On the one hand, he didn't want to spend every waking hour reliving the trauma, but on the other hand, he needed to know just what happened with the GPIRB and try to save other sailors from a similar fate. The fear, the confusion, and the brush with death also need reflection, time, and space. Like broken ribs, they cannot be ignored. Well-intentioned people say it's time to move on, but those who experience trauma firsthand know that's easy to say but hard to do.

JP did provide some comfort to the families of the sailors on the *Flying Colours*. After he finished writing up the final log of the *Sean Seamour II*, he sent it to Captain McBride of the Coast Guard, and he asked permission to share it with the families of the four young people lost at sea. They would never be able to know what occurred in that early hurricane, but JP's log described what it was like to be at sea during the height of the storm. Some of the families contacted JP, and he helped them understand what might have happened to their sons and daughters.

The next two years were difficult ones for JP. His investigation consumed him; he was suffering from sleepless nights and some anxious days. He had left the business world to restore a fourteenth-century home and gardens in the South of France, yet he wasn't feeling the joy he expected while working on his hilltop home.

His wife, Mayke, knew JP was hurting and suggested he work out his problems with a therapist. Rudy, who was in frequent contact with JP, encouraged him to seek healing for post-traumatic stress disorder. Finally, two years after the accident, he decided to try counseling. The therapy unleashed a flood of emotions. It was difficult but necessary, showing JP that he needed to face the compartmentalized aspects of his life. He knew he had stored away many traumatic events into "boxes tucked away on shelves." Now he had to rip open each of those boxes and examine the contents. It was at this point that JP started working on a manuscript about his life.

JP describes the next months as follows:

Through writing and discussions, I acknowledged what a tremendous blow it was to lose the *Sean Seamour II*. Not just for myself but for Mayke and for what we had built together. It was really home to her. When we lived in Port Grimaud with her studio in the house and our boat tied up in front, in the evening we would often sleep on board. And weekend lines were cast and we would be out to sea.

Sean Seamour II was a compilation of fifteen years of life and dreams; she was the descendant of *Lou Pantai,* the first boat of my first crossing and turning point of my life. She held all of my treasures and memories of the past; there was everything in there, from old coin collections, original bills of lading dating as far back as 1687, to personal memorabilia, a lifetime of sailing paraphernalia and equipment. She was an accomplishment I lost, and with it the faded dream since the age of fourteen to circumnavigate the world. But I was alive and had so much to live for. I wondered why the irritability and anxiety?

The therapist explained that in extreme cases in which the instincts for self-preservation are triggered from our innermost depths, like the ones I experienced during the storm, the cerebral cortex, a remnant from our reptilian evolutionary past, produces cerebral cortisol. In some people, like myself, the cortisol stays elevated even after the extreme event is over. The therapy eventually allowed me to reclaim my natural behavior and come to terms with the accident, as well as unburden past problems, particularly the abuse by my father.

I began to make positive changes in both perspective and priorities. First and foremost, I no longer wear a watch. Time is too precious to count it. So now I live in my time and a newfound patience.

Encountering death for the second time, staring you in the eye, to be reconciled that it is your time to go, has made me appreciate the little moments in life. Every day I still learn that most of the things that upset us are not worth the aggravation. I learn to let them go or ignore them. Our lives are so imprinted with frenetic needs and materialistic values that it can be hard to shake that kind of thinking. I've learned nothing is very important, yet each day is so important.

The last few years of my life have been the very best: to learn to appreciate the love I share with Mayke and our moments together. Her initial fury that I put myself in harm's way subsided once she came to accept there was no hubris in my quest, to understand that our attractions to the sea are parallel; to her awe and need for contemplation, there is my need for communion with this force of nature. Yet it has taken me the years since these events to answer her nagging question: Why undertake the challenge when life is at your fingertips?

It is because I am a lone romantic. The sea was and remains the medium of my emancipation. When I was ten, it became my safe conduit from storms of the recent past, enabling me to discover and measure my abilities. Then the exhilarated adolescent braved the elements in his quest for self. Humility would come later, and with it, the strength derived from respect for and kinship with the omnipresent forces of nature. It is that strength and the dedication of four extraordinary men that allow my words today.

(To assist other sailors, JP has posted "Lessons Learned" on his website at www.artseaprovence.com.)

RUDY SNEL

It takes a certain kind of person to cross the Atlantic Ocean in a forty-four-foot sailboat with two strangers. Most of us would not do it, even if well paid. Rudy, however, wasn't going to sit idly through his retirement before the ill-fated trip on the *Sean Seamour II;* nor has he become a couch potato after it. He continues to travel and try new adventures, and perhaps one day he will complete the transatlantic crossing.

After the accident, Rudy traveled back to Elizabeth City and visited with the helicopter crew who saved his life. In Washington, he recounted his survival story in a presentation to the Coast Guard and the administrators and member country representatives of the International Satellite System (COSPAS-SARSAT) that helped in his rescue. His goal was to share what he learned so that others might avoid such an ordeal and to give thanks for all those people behind the scenes who helped with his rescue. Since then, thanks to JP's efforts, the NOAA has tightened the registration procedure for EPIRBs, which may save other sailors from the hazard of duplicate serial numbers.

Rudy has become good friends with Drew Dazzo and Scott Higgins, visiting them and staying in touch. When Drew was awarded the Star of Courage by the Canadian Government, both he and Scott, as well as Nevada, stayed at Rudy's Ottawa home and enjoyed Canadian hospitality.

Rudy reflects on his survival at sea with humility and gratitude, expressed in the following paragraph.

EPILOGUE

In the days after our rescue, when JP, Ben, and I traveled together on our way home, we counted at least six things that, if any one of them had been even slightly different, we would not have survived. Thanks to JP's enormously determined, caring, and competent nature, as well as the daring and phenomenal skill of the USCG, we did survive. Sitting in what was left of the life raft, looking at the scenery while being certain that death was at most a few hours away, along with trying to look after JP when at times I was not sure he was alive, and being in an upside-down boat at night in an incredible storm have left their mark. Counseling for PTSD has helped explain some of the aftermath. I was able to deal with our situation calmly and rationally because, according to the psychiatrist, I was in a dissociative state. Currently, even though the experience has made me more appreciative of life's moments, trivial things can be very irritating. Life will never be quite the same. My desire to sail across the Atlantic is still there. The days of sailing with JP and Ben before the storm were great! There was a relaxing sense of freedom despite being confined to a forty-four-foot boat. This surely is the norm.

DREW DAZZO (RESCUE SWIMMER)

Drew Dazzo received the Canadian Star of Courage for saving the life of Rudy Snel. Drew is only the third American recipient of the award, which is similar to the American Medal of Honor. He is still a rescue swimmer, saving lives.

SCOTT HIGGINS (FLIGHT MECHANIC)

Scott is now serving from Cape Cod Air Station. Even on training missions, he seems to be involved in SARs. In August 2011 he was on a nighttime gunnery training mission when he and the Jayhawk helicopter crew he was flying with saw a private plane take off and then crash into the woods and erupt into a ball of fire. The crew was able to put the helicopter down about two hundred feet from the crash site. Higgins ran to the plane and found a woman in critical condition. Emergency workers from the airport arrived and decided that carrying the woman out on foot might further injure her. The Coast Guard helicopter crew returned to their aircraft and did a basket hoist to get her out of the woods and then transferred her to a MedFlight.

GEOFF PAGELS (SAR HEADQUARTERS)

May 7, 2007, will forever be etched in my mind. It was without a doubt the most epic day I have ever stood duty as a search and rescue controller at the Fifth District Command Center. I still can recall feeling as though I answered the telephone two hundred times that day. I can also recall the commanding officer of Sector North Carolina calling me and Lieutenant Katie Moretti, my watch partner, at the end of watch telling us, "We done good!" We saved nine people that day from three separate cases. We had multiple HC-130 Hercules and multiple MH-60 Jayhawk launches that day, which just doesn't happen during the regular course of Coast Guard business. For the *Flying Colours,* we initiated what I perceive as the largest Coast Guard response since the space shuttle *Challenger* recovery effort, which I was also a part of while serving on the USCGC *Dallas* as a young quartermaster. During the *Flying Colours* search, we ended up searching an area about the size of Texas, with over two hundred hours of aircraft on-scene time. Again, this simply does not happen, but we were committed to finding the *Flying Colours* and her crew. The search was ongoing for a week. I stood duty during the search over three twelve-hour shifts. Never in my fifteen years of experience as a search and rescue controller have I seen such dedication, steadfastness, and personal commitment by all the involved search units to finding a missing group of people. Although the final outcome was unfortunate, this was truly an unprecedented effort by all of the Coast Guardsmen, aviators, and cutters who searched for the *Flying Colours* and her crew.

As I get older and as each year goes by, the tragedy of the *Flying Colours* has left an emotional scar on my psyche. I extend to the family and friends of the *Flying Colours* crew my heartfelt compassion and condolences on the loss of their loved ones.

EPILOGUE

NEVADA SMITH (HELICOPTER PILOT)

Nevada and Rudy have stayed in touch since the rescue and have had two visits. Rudy came to Elizabeth City to see the USCG's awards ceremony in December 2008, and Nevada went to Ottawa for Drew's Star of Courage ceremony in February 2010.

Nevada has had many SAR cases during his "duty standing" years between 1995 and 2008. He considers the May 7 rescues equal to the three sorties he flew over New Orleans in which he rescued more than 130 victims after Hurricane Katrina.

In the spring of 2010 Nevada commissioned an artist to paint *Star of Courage*, which depicts Drew surrounded by the mountainous waves as Rudy is hoisted to the helicopter. Scott is seen leaning out of the helicopter while Ben remains in the raft, awaiting his turn in the basket. The C-130 is in the background, keeping a vigilant watch. The painting is on the largest canvas that the artist, Kris Stoll, had access to in Chesapeake, Virginia. Mrs. Stoll worked on it for more than six months. The painting has been a big hit at Coast Guard gatherings. Each of the survivors and rescuers has received a print, and one currently hangs near the bell that owners and survivors of the sailing vessel *Illusion* presented to the D5 Command Center.

Having a painting done of a rescue had been on Nevada's bucket list since he was a kid. Back then, he used to ride his bike to a Ben Franklin store in Morrisonville, Illinois, and admire the pictures on the boxes of plastic model airplanes depicting fighters and bombers in dramatic scenes. He always thought, *Someday I'll be in a painting like that.*

In early 2012 Nevada received orders to be the air operations officer at Sector Columbia River in Oregon.

DANE AND JENIFER CLARK
(GULF STREAM EXPERTS)

To experience the majestic royal blue waters of the Gulf Stream on a calm, warm spring day is an awe-inspiring adventure. There you observe the swirling Sargasso weed lines that define the sharp edge between the greenish-turquoise waters of the Atlantic Continental Shelf and the brilliant blue waters of the Gulf Stream. But during ocean storms, the Gulf Stream is transformed into huge steep mountains of white frothy foam—a nightmare for mariners! These peaks of ocean energy merge to form deadly and monstrous waves—the so-called rogue wave. These tower above the waves around them, and unlike the earthquake-generated tsunami wave, rogues are often short-lived and localized and difficult to predict.

Because of the *Flying Colours* tragedy, and information gathered from the 2005 *Norwegian Dawn* cruise ship incident, Dane and Jenifer were motivated to begin looking for a method to better forecast these killer storms. This work led to the development of the Gulf Stream Hazard Scale in 2008. The Clarks then teamed with representatives of the National Weather Service (NWS) Ocean Prediction Center to further refine and plan how this scale can be used to improve marine forecasts along the East Coast of the U.S. In 2012 the NWS is planning to initiate an experimental product that will use the scale to enhance the predictions of dangerous ocean wave conditions. The product is expected to provide critical information to the marine community that will potentially save lives and property for vessels encountering major East Coast storms.

AARON NELSON (COPILOT)

I had the pleasure of meeting Rudy in 2007, and one thing I remember is he thanked me repeatedly for participating in his rescue. At the time, I couldn't completely comprehend his vantage point—after all, I was just doing my job. In early 2011, I was diagnosed with a primary brain tumor. The initial prognosis wasn't that great, but I did get lucky—I had the great fortune of being treated by Dr. Allan Friedman at Duke University Hospital in Durham. By the grace of God, and Dr. Friedman's incredible talents, I'm doing well. I think of Dr. Friedman as a true "angel among us," and I can't possibly thank him enough! Perhaps I can more closely relate to the feelings of Rudy and the rest of the crew. It's easy to think of the helicopter crew—or doctor, in my case—as the hero. But it's also important to recognize that it's a team effort. Without the Coast Guard team, the end result could have been much different on this SAR case. I'm just glad I was able to help them out, and I'm happy they're all doing well. I wish them the best in life. I may someday return to flying (crossed fingers), but for now the Coast Guard is moving me to the District 9 Command Center in Cleveland, Ohio, where I'll coordinate search and rescue efforts on the Great Lakes. To Rudy, Ben, and JP, Godspeed.

EDWARD W. AHLSTRAND (C-130 PILOT)

Following my tour at U.S. Coast Guard Air Station Elizabeth City, North Carolina, I was transferred to Coast Guard Air Station Barbers Point, Hawaii, where I have been the last four years. While I have flown and conducted missions, including SAR, out of remote islands that most people can only dream about, I have never prosecuted a SAR case as unique and memorable as that of the *Sean Seamour II*.

I had the pleasure of meeting Rudy Snel before departing North Carolina in 2008. Rudy and his son came down from Canada for the awards presentation at the air station. The meeting, which my wife attended, was memorable on several levels. I laughed when Rudy casually mentioned how hope was restored when we made our first pass over them, believing they had been found. His eyes grew as big as quarters when I informed him that we in fact didn't locate the raft until much later, after making multiple passes over the EPIRB signal; he didn't find that as funny as my wife and I did. Following this, Rudy and his son recounted their experiences as both the rescued and the family member eagerly hoping for good news and the return of a loved one. My wife listened intently. She later told me that she had never before truly realized the significance of what we did and what it meant to others. This, as much as anything, made it worth it.

I have stayed in touch with most of the crew. Paul Beavis and I have stayed close and will find ourselves neighbors again as we are both doing staff tours in Washington, D.C. Marcus Jones and I keep in touch every so often by e-mail. In all likelihood we will be stationed together again in the future and pick up where we left off.

EPILOGUE

Ryan Cantu, Stacy Sorenson, and I are stationed in Hawaii and see each other daily. We often discuss the *Sean Seamour II* case. How can we not?

Video of the rescue of Rudy, Ben, and JP can be found on YouTube, "A Storm Too Soon."

TRIBUTE TO THE CREW OF
THE *FLYING COLOURS*
WRITTEN BY THEIR PARENTS

RHIANNON BORISOFF

Rhiannon was not a typical only child. She was always considerate and sensitive toward others. She grew up with four generations of hundred-pound yellow Labs that she was very close to. Her love of animals grew throughout her life. One of her many quotes was "Animals are the greatest teachers of unconditional love."

Her best friends said she was the happiest person they knew, always smiling. She had a unique sense of humor, often laughing at things that most people probably wouldn't find funny. Almost all photos of her show a beaming smile. She wanted everyone around her to be happy. Rhiannon wanted more than anything to be part of something, and to be and feel loved. She loved life and could make even the most boring event enjoyable with her presence. She had an energy and life about her, and defined "free spirit."

She was very tough physically and mentally and did not know the meaning of quitting. She had wisdom and courage beyond her years.

Rhiannon loved knowledge and was constantly in a learning mode. She earned a 4.0 GPA in marine biology in college. She loved everything nautical. Ocean, sun, beach, salt air, lighthouses, white sand, foghorns, and the sound of ropes hitting masts. She spent almost every summer in New England, near the beaches and ocean. She loved astronomy and watching the night sky. Writing and music were her ongoing escapes. "Love" was the word that was always used in her writing and the music she listened to. She prized words and quotes that illustrated what was most important in her life. A quote she used often was "What defines us is how we rise after falling."

Rhiannon was very sentimental. She would save ticket stubs from movies, cards from bouquets of flowers, seashells, bottle caps, rocks, letters, postcards. She was grateful for everything and always expressed gratitude for anything that was done for her.

Rhiannon was attending Animal Behavior College to be a dog trainer and was a volunteer at the Potter League Shelter in Middletown, Rhode Island. We feel she would have been the next "dog whisperer."

Rhiannon left us all too soon. We all miss her so much. We hope she is where the sand is white, the water turquoise, and where the stars go blue.

I Will Be (a poem by Rhiannon Borisoff)
I will be
a woman, proud, and uncompromising.
I understand
that life will be what you make it,
that sometimes the coat of many colors
that marks your achievements brightly, blends only
to the loneliest of grey.

JASON FRANKS

Jason Ernest Franks was born on February 10, 1973, in Dartmouth, England. Jason's first passion was writing, and his second was sailing. He started sailing at the age of ten in England on the River Dart. He came to America with his mother in 1985, graduated from high school, attended Fordham College, and graduated from Florida State University. Jason moved to San Diego, where he taught sailing at the San Diego Yacht Club and earned his captain's license. In 2002 he moved to Newport, Rhode Island, to be close to his family and continue his sailing career. After transatlantic crossings, he captained the *Rum Runner, Madeline, Spirit of Newport,* and other power and sailing vessels hailing from Newport. Jason's last berth was as the captain of the eighty-five-foot sailing vessel *Adventurous.* He also taught special education in the Newport public school system.

Jason received a call from his friend Captain Patrick "Trey" Topping in April 2007, asking for his help in bringing the *Flying Colours* from St. Thomas to Annapolis, Maryland. Jason, after receiving permission from the owner of the *Adventurous,* flew to St. Thomas to help his friend. They were never heard from again, lost in the first named storm, Andrea, approximately 187 miles southeast of the Carolinas.

Jason was loved and a friend to all. He is especially missed by his mother and father, Ron and Carol Dale, his brother, Tony, and his black dog, King.

CHRISTINE GRINAVIC

Christine Grinavic was working in the spring of 2007 as a crew member with her "other family," on the sailboat *Arabella,* based in St. Thomas and Newport. They traveled around the Caribbean and Martha's Vineyard. She had last been home in December 2006 for her beloved nana's funeral, where she delivered a special eulogy and then went back to her work at sea. She loved the sea. She had originally intended to come home to New England with the *Arabella* but was offered the opportunity to "crew" with friends on the *Flying Colours.* That would mean she could be home for Mother's Day. "I'll be your present this year, Mom," she said on the phone to her mother. "I know you are missing Nana."

Christine loved traveling around the world and had traveled to five continents. She impressed everyone who ever met her with her enthusiasm for life and extremely positive attitude. She had no patience for those she deemed to be a "Bitter Betty" or "Gloomy Gus." That philosophy has helped her mom to go forward with the positive attitude Christine would demand.

She was the only child of Mary and James Grinavic. Her dad died suddenly, of a heart attack, five weeks after their treasured daughter was reported missing at sea. Some think that he died of a broken heart. The Coast Guard conducted a massive search of the Atlantic with no sign of the *Flying Colours* or her sailors. It took a very long time for the families and friends of the four missing sailors to accept the reality that their loved ones were not drifting at sea and would never come home.

Christine had a great philosophy of how to live life. This is an excerpt from an essay she wrote, about the period when she had "dropped out" of college (with a 3.87 GPA!). She later achieved a degree from University of Rhode Island.

> And I realized that being happy is the most important thing in life. Because life is precious, and even a few months ought not to be wasted. No time should be wasted. You are never stuck. You just can't be afraid of a jump.
>
> . . . So, I am going home for some time off . . . Yes, I'll finish my degree, I just don't know where or when yet . . . I'll finish in a way that's right for me. Not a way that is tailored for others. There's no sense in making a tight jacket fit when there's lots of coats in this world. Everyone ought to wear one that is comfortable . . .

She was so very wise, and lived her life well, and is very much missed by many.

TREY TOPPING

Patrick Joseph Topping III (Trey to all who knew him) was the captain of *Flying Colours*. Trey, with his quick wit, sharp intellect, Southern charm, and good looks, had it all and lived more in his thirty-nine years than most do in eighty. He possessed an adventurous spirit and took great pride in pursuing his passions. Trey spent his life cultivating his many talents and always earned his living doing what he loved, whether that was cycling, woodworking, or sailing. He was an avid reader, a creative writer, an amazing storyteller, and a talented photographer.

Trey loved to sail. He agreed with the description that sailing is "long periods of boredom punctuated by moments of sheer terror." In the off-seasons, when he wasn't sailing or traveling, Trey put his woodworking skills to work restoring the historic homes of Newport and building furniture. He was a master craftsman, and as in most things, he was self-taught.

When not sailing, Trey would throw on his backpack and take extended trips to exotic places. Over the years he traveled extensively in Asia (China, Burma, Kashmir, Thailand, Tibet, Nepal, and India), northern Africa, South America, Central America, and Southern Europe. He was especially drawn to India, which he visited twice, with plans to return and pursue his interest in photography. Trey loved to travel and didn't shy away from visiting places others might avoid, whether it was climbing the Himalayas, cycling through Africa, working as a movie extra in India, or even spending a night in a Bolivian jail after unsuccessfully haggling with a water-taxi driver. He lived in a hut with Burmese Indians, in the home of a Moroccan sugar merchant, and on a houseboat in war-torn Kashmir. His travels were truly adventures in every sense of the word, and they all became fodder for the stories he loved to tell.

He enjoyed traveling solo on his bicycle, once riding up the Pacific Coast Highway from San Diego to Seattle and on to Utah. His last trip abroad was a two-month, two-thousand-mile bicycling odyssey across Southern Europe, which he chronicled in his blog, www.crazyguyonabike.com. He wrote, "My pride in life is to forever remain true to my nature regardless of what others may be doing." Trey *was* true to himself and lived his life passionately.

Trey was a son, a brother, an uncle, and a friend. He loved his family and his friends. He is loved and missed by all who knew him.

AUTHOR'S NOTE AND ACKNOWLEDGMENTS

This book all started with a photo. I had seen an amazing photograph culled from the video shot by Nevada Smith that showed JP's life raft in a seventy-foot wave. My curiosity was piqued: Did the people in the raft survive? And if so, how in the world were they rescued? I wasn't planning to write a book, but Nevada changed that.

Nevada and I corresponded by e-mail and then by phone. As he recounted the rescue of the crew from the *Sean Seamour II* and shared more images with me, I became more and more interested, knowing this story had all the twists and turns I enjoy investigating. Best of all, Nevada was as patient as he was intelligent, answering my many questions, painting a vivid picture of the rescue and the people involved. And so my first thank-you is to Nevada—he was the perfect partner to get me started when I contacted him in July 2007, and he was still helping me when I completed the writing five years later. (Nevada, I have a copy of our first e-mail, in which you wrote, "Here are some additional pictures. Are you working on another project?" Little did I know that one e-mail would send me on a five-year mission!)

Having Nevada in my corner was a good start, but the next step was critical. Would the survivors want to talk about such a traumatic experience? The first name I was given was Rudy Snel's, and when I contacted him, he was a true gentleman. I knew we would work well together. It wasn't easy for him to dive back into the storm and relive those terrible hours, but he thought the story needed to be told, and he felt other mariners' lives might someday be saved by the lessons learned from his accident. One of my fondest memories from the project is the evening when Rudy and the flight mechanic Scott Higgins came to my house after they had been out fishing on the ocean. The three of us sat down around my porch table, and Rudy described what happened on the sailboat before the helicopter crew located the raft. Neither Scott nor I had heard all the various details of the courageous acts performed by JP, and for an hour I just let my tape recorder run while Scott and I sat mesmerized.

In Rudy's section of the epilogue, he mentions that he counted six different instances in which he would have died had an event happened just slightly differently. I found myself doing the same thing as I was writing the book: counting the times when luck, or fate, had to intervene for any chance at survival. I found ten turning points where the outcome could have been disaster if an event had not gone exactly as it had or happened just a second or two later. An example is when Rudy tried to shoot a flare from the raft. Out of three flares, the first two were duds, and the wind blew the third and final flare sideways into a wave. C-130 crewman Marcus Jones told me that he saw that flare only for a split second, and if it hadn't been seen, he's not sure they would have found the raft.

I contacted Ben after Rudy, and we had a good talk on Skype, as he was working in Bahrain. We never had an opportunity to meet, but he answered my questions via e-mail during the writing process. Ben once told me that he tries not to think too much about the accident because he doesn't want it to define him, and I did my best to respect that and limit my questions and probing. Ben, thank you for your time on a book that you were never pushing for.

Because the *Sean Seamour II* was JP's boat, and because of his tumultuous childhood, he bore the brunt of my detective work and probably some pretty dumb questions. But JP made my job so much easier by graciously sending me a manuscript he was writing about his life. This helped get me up to speed before we started communicating in earnest. Then JP invited me to visit him in France to continue our discussions. I asked my daughter Kristin to join me and help with the research and also to extend our trip into Italy. She jumped at the chance. Because of her partnership—as well as JP's and Mayke's hospitality—I had the trip of a lifetime. During our visit, I observed just how resourceful JP is as I viewed his handiwork restoring his fourteenth-century stone home. He and Mayke have carved out a wonderful life. It was a pleasure to know that after all the turmoil in JP's earlier years, he has now found peace.

Much of JP's work is outdoors, building stone walls, clearing garden plots, and cutting and splitting wood used to heat his home. Yet somehow he has time for the sea. He took Kristin and me out in the Gulf of Saint-Tropez on his new boat, the *Sean Seamour III,* where I conducted part of our interview after a swim. Because we were on a sailboat, he could show me exactly what was happening to his vessel during the storm, such as how he was able to free the raft from the mast and spreader. I was able to take pictures, draw illustrations, and tape-record JP's comments, all invaluable when trying to reconstruct the desperate hours during the first two knockdowns.

I have three memories of that trip that will always stay with me. The first was when JP showed me the back alleys of Saint-Tropez where he roamed as a boy, a loner but free from his father. He explained in *A Storm Too Soon* how the ocean almost took his life but how it also was his refuge when he began sailing and venturing farther and farther out to sea. My second memory is of the wonderful dinners we had outside in the courtyard at JP's house. We not only continued fleshing out the book, with tips from Mayke and Kristin, but we also laughed and talked about a thousand other things. And my final memory involves the last day of our visit, when I insisted on accompanying JP up the mountain to gather stones to build the pillars that would support the gate into his vegetable garden. We took his tractor up the slopes and filled its bed with flat stones. It was a hot day in the sun, but the work was enjoyable, the views uplifting, and the companionship comfortable. It gave me a glimpse into JP's new life, and it was clearly a balanced one, filled with happiness and gratitude. He deserves it.

A year after that trip, JP came to New England to help his stepmother, Betty, and he stayed with me a couple days. I remember showing JP around my home and apologizing for the clutter, saying someday soon I would break myself of my pack rat ways. JP responded, "Being a pack rat saved my life," meaning that if he hadn't kept the old EPIRB on the *Sean Seamour II,* he wouldn't be alive today. The highlight of the visit was when Rudy came down from Canada and the three of us had dinner. The book was well on its way, and we cleared up a couple of loose ends. I was surprised how the two men's memories were in perfect sync, and glad to see that they had not lost their sense of humor because of the post-traumatic stress they endured. They were both able to talk about the accident much more openly than when I first approached them.

This is my second book about survival during a storm in the Gulf Stream, and it prompted me to consider the stories we hear about the Bermuda Triangle. Some who believe that something mysterious is going on in the Bermuda Triangle have expanded its area all the way up to New Jersey. They ask why some boats and aircraft have disappeared without a trace, and they attribute it to paranormal or extraterrestrial influence. But for the real reason, they should look no farther than the Gulf Stream. Its warm waters can create its own microclimate, especially when there are downdrafts of cold air, causing hazards for low-flying aircraft. Boats large and small face another hazard in or near the Gulf Stream when storms funneling winds out of a northerly direction create waves that run counter to the current. As Gulf Stream experts Dane and Jenifer Clark point out, this can lead to the dreaded rogue wave. We have seen time and again how these waves can surprise a crew and swallow a boat whole, sending it to the bottom of the sea in a matter of seconds or minutes. This might explain why some vessels in the so-called Bermuda Triangle vanish with no Mayday, while vessels in other areas, hit by the same storm, ride it out in fine shape. And as JP learned, your boat doesn't have to be in the Stream to be impacted. Its warm-water eddies, reaching out like fat tentacles, can also ensnare a boat in extreme waves.

I'm often asked to speak at yacht clubs, Coast Guard stations, and other military groups, and the hosts generally assume I once served in the Coast Guard. I haven't. Nor am I a sailor. I think these two facts have assisted me greatly in crafting my ocean survival books, because I'm writing for the general public, and I want the story to be character-driven rather than focusing too much on the inner workings of the Coast Guard or of sailing. My primary goal when writing is to keep the book fast-paced, and to do that I try not to burden the reader with minutiae but, rather, to weave in select details so he or she can visualize what is happening. Copilot Aaron Nelson was especially good at simplifying what happened during the rescue yet painting a vivid picture for me.

There were many people who assisted me in this project, and I want to thank those I have yet to mention, in no particular order. From the Coast Guard, I'd like to acknowledge Jeremy Davis, Jason Trichler, Steven Banks, Brian Avelsgard, Charles Fosse, Dan Molthen, Andy Clayton, Mike Ackermann, Dan Cancetty, David McBride, Geoff Pagels, Ed Ahlstrand, Stacy Sorenson, Marcus Jones, Paul Beavis, Casey Green, Ryan Cantu, Tasha Hood, Scott Walden, Justin Cimbak, Drew Dazzo, Steve Fischer, Bill Coty, Doug Atkins, Roberto Torres, and a big thank-you to the behind-the-scenes Coasties who provide support for the rescuers.

Outside the Coast Guard, a myriad of people inspired or helped me, and they include: Betty de Lutz, Ron Burd, Mayke Sassen, Robin Lee Graham, Jenifer and Dane Clark, Peter Reich, Andy Reeve, Mary Grinavic, Diana Rogers, Carol Dale, Michael Borisoff, Steven Callahan, John Clayman, and Luke Wiedman (future rescue swimmer!).

At Simon & Schuster, I'd like to thank Colin Harrison, who has now done a superb job guiding four of my manuscripts into finished books. Working with Colin is a dedicated team that includes Kelsey Smith, Sophie Vershbow, and Beth Thomas.

Other writers whose work helped in my research include Doug Campbell at *Soundings* magazine, who first wrote about the storm; William MacLeish, who wrote about the Gulf Stream; Robin Lee Graham, who wrote about his solo voyage; and the USCG Historian's Office.

I'd also like to thank the readers who have shared kind words and come to my presentations. Those gestures give me energy.

ABOUT THE AUTHOR

Michael Tougias is a versatile author and coauthor of twenty books. His best-selling book *Fatal Forecast: An Incredible True Tale of Disaster and Survival at Sea* was praised by the *Los Angeles Times* as "a breathtaking book . . . [Tougias] spins a marvelous and terrifying yarn." His earlier book, *Ten Hours Until Dawn: The True Story of Heroism and Tragedy Aboard the Can Do* was praised by *Booklist* "as the best story of peril at sea since *The Perfect Storm*." This book, about a sea rescue during the blizzard of 1978, was selected by the American Library Association as an editor's choice—one of the top books of the year.

Tougias and coauthor Casey Sherman teamed up and wrote a combination history/ocean rescue story titled *The Finest Hours: The True Story of the U.S. Coast Guard's Most Daring Sea Rescue.* This drama occurred in 1952 off the coast of Cape Cod when two oil tankers, in the grip of a nor'easter, were split in half and eighty-four lives were in jeopardy. The Disney Corporation is currently making a movie based on this book.

On a lighter note, Tougias's award-winning humor book *There's a Porcupine in My Outhouse: Misadventures of a Mountain Man Wannabe* was selected by the Independent Book Publishers Association as the best nature book of the year. The author has also written for more than two hundred diverse publications, including the *New York Times, Field & Stream, Fine Gardening,* and the *Boston Globe.* He is currently working on a book titled *Derek's Gift: A True Story of Love, Courage and Lessons Learned.*

Tougias has prepared slide lectures for all his books, including *A Storm Too Soon,* and his lecture schedule is posted on his website at

ABOUT THE AUTHOR

www.michaeltougias.com (interested organizations can contact him at michaeltougias@yahoo.com).

The author also has an archive of maritime rescue articles and personal stories on his blog, michaeltougias.wordpress.com, and he has an author page on Facebook at Michael J. Tougias.

Through research into dozens of survival stories, Tougias has prepared an inspirational lecture for businesses and organizations titled "Survival Lessons: Peak Performance and Decision-making Under Pressure." Tougias describes this presentation as "an uplifting way to learn some practical strategies and mind-sets for achieving difficult goals from those who have survived against all odds." He has given the presentation across the country for all types of organizations, including General Dynamics, International Administrative Association, the Massachusetts School Library Association, New York University's Surgeons' Round Table, Lincoln Financial Services, Goodwin Procter LLP, the United States Coast Guard, and many more. For more details, see www.michaeltougias.com.

SUMMARY OF MICHAEL J. TOUGIAS'S LATEST BOOKS

The Finest Hours: The True Story of the
U.S. Coast Guard's Most Daring Sea Rescue
(coauthored with Casey Sherman)

On February 18, 1952, an astonishing maritime event began when a ferocious nor'easter split in half a five-hundred-foot-long oil tanker, the *Pendleton,* approximately one mile off the coast of Cape Cod, Massachusetts. Incredibly, just twenty miles away, a second oil tanker, the *Fort Mercer,* also split in half. On both fractured tankers, men were trapped on the severed bows and sterns, and all four sections were sinking in sixty-foot seas. Thus began a life-and-death drama of survival, heroism, and tragedy. Of the eighty-four seamen aboard the tankers, seventy would be rescued and fourteen would lose their lives.

Going to the rescue of the *Pendleton*'s stern section were four young Coast Guardsmen in a thirty-six-foot lifeboat—a potential suicide mission in such a small vessel. Standing between the men and their mission were towering waves that reached seventy feet, blinding snow, and one of the most dangerous shoals in the world, the dreaded Chatham Bar. The waters along the outer arm of Cape Cod are called the graveyard of the Atlantic for good reason, yet this rescue defied all odds when thirty-two survivors were crammed into the tiny lifeboat and brought to safety. (Coast Guard officials later said that "the rescue is unparalleled in the entire annals of maritime history.")

Several cutters and small boats raced to the sinking sections of the *Fort Mercer,* and valiant rescue attempts were undertaken: some successful, some not. (An interview with Michael Tougias and photos of the disaster unfolding can be found on YouTube under "Finest Hours—Adam Knee, producer.")

"A blockbuster account of tragedy at sea . . . gives a you-are-there feel."

—*The Providence Journal*

"A gripping read!"

—James Bradley, author of *Flags of Our Fathers*

Overboard!:
A True Blue-water Odyssey of Disaster and Survival

The latest nerve-wracking maritime disaster tale from the masterful author of *Fatal Forecast* and *The Finest Hours*. Michael Tougias has left countless readers breathless with his suspense-packed, nail-biting disaster-at-sea narratives. And now one of the survivors of a perilous tale has sought Tougias out to tell his terrifying story, for the first time described in *Overboard!*

In early May 2005 Captain Tom Tighe and first mate Loch Reidy of the sailboat *Almeisan* welcomed three new crew members for a five-day voyage from Connecticut to Bermuda. While Tighe and Reidy had made the journey countless times, the rest of the crew wanted to learn about offshore sailing—and were looking for adventure. Four days into their voyage, they got one—but nothing that they had expected or had any training to handle. A massive storm struck, sweeping Tighe and Reidy from the boat. The remaining crew members somehow managed to stay aboard the vessel as it was torn apart by wind and water. *Overboard!* follows the simultaneous desperate struggles of boat passengers and the captain and first mate fighting for their lives in the sea. (An interview with the author and survivors, along with actual footage from the storm, can be found on YouTube under "Michael Tougias—Overboard Part I, II, III.")

> "A heart-pounding account of the storm that tore apart a forty-five-foot sailboat. Author Michael Tougias is the master of the weather-related disaster book."
>
> —*The Boston Globe*
>
> "*Overboard!* is a beautiful story deserving of a good cry."
>
> —Gatehouse News Service
>
> "Tougias has a knack for weaving thoroughly absorbing stories—adventure fans need this one!"
>
> —*Booklist*

Fatal Forecast: An Incredible True Tale of
Disaster and Survival at Sea

On a cold November day in 1980, two fishing vessels, the *Fair Wind*
and the *Sea Fever,* set out from Cape Cod to catch offshore lobsters
at Georges Bank. The National Weather Service had forecast typical fall weather in the area for the next three days—even though the
organization knew that its only weather buoy at Georges Bank was
malfunctioning. Soon after the boats reached the fishing ground,
they were hit with hurricane-force winds and massive sixty-foot
waves that battered the boats for hours. The captains and crews
struggled heroically to keep their vessels afloat in the unrelent-
ing storm. One monstrous wave of ninety to a hundred feet soon
capsized the *Fair Wind,* trapping the crew inside. Meanwhile, on the
Sea Fever, Captain Peter Brown (whose father owned the *Andrea Gail*
of *The Perfect Storm* fame) did his best to ride out the storm, but a
giant wave blew out one side of the pilothouse, sending a crew
member into the churning ocean.

Meticulously researched and vividly told, *Fatal Forecast* is first and
foremost a tale of miraculous survival. Most amazing is the story
of Ernie Hazard, who had managed to crawl inside a tiny inflatable
life raft, only to be repeatedly thrown into the ocean as he fought
to endure more than fifty hours adrift in the storm-tossed seas. By
turns tragic, thrilling, and inspiring, Ernie's story deserves a place
among the greatest survival tales ever told.

As gripping and harrowing as *The Perfect Storm* but with a miracle ending, *Fatal Forecast* is an unforgettable true story about the
collision of two spectacular forces: the brutality of nature and the
human will to survive.

"Tougias skillfully submerges us in this storm and spins a marvelous and terrifying yarn. He makes us fight alongside Ernie
Hazard and cheer as he is saved . . . a breathtaking book."

—*Los Angeles Times*

"Ernie Hazard's experiences, as related by Tougias, deserve a
place as a classic of sea survival history."

—*The Boston Globe*

"Tougias spins a dramatic saga. . . . [He] has written eighteen
books and this is among his most gripping."

—*National Geographic Adventure*